# THE CELESTIAL KEY TO THE VEDAS

## Discovering the Origins of the World's Oldest Civilization

B. G. Sidharth

To Dr Daphne & Tony with regards

Inner Traditions
Rochester, Vermont

Inner Traditions International
One Park Street
Rochester, Vermont 05767
www.InnerTraditions.com



**Library of Congress Cataloging-in-Publication Data**

Sidharth, B. G. (Burra Gautam), 1948–
The celestial key to the vedas : discovering the origins of the world's oldest civilization / B.G. Sidharth.
p. cm.
Includes index.
ISBN 0-89281-753-4 (alk. paper)
1. Astronomy in the Vedas. 2. Vedas. Ṛgveda—Criticism, interpretation, etc. 3. Astronomy—Religious aspects—Hinduism. 4. Civilization, Hindu. I. Title.
BL1112.47.S57 1999
294.5'921046—dc21 99-20106
CIP

Printed and bound in Canada

10 9 8 7 6 5 4 3 2 1

This book was typeset in Times with Kyrebrannog used as a display face.

*Dedicated to the memory of my parents*

# CONTENTS


| | | |
|---|---|---|
| | Introduction | 1 |
| 1. | The Case for Indian Astronomy | 15 |
| 2. | The Astronomy of the Hindus | 23 |
| 3. | The Heliocentric Theory in the Ṛg Veda | 39 |
| 4. | Astronomy in the Ṛg Veda | 45 |
| 5. | The Unmythical Purāṇas: A Study in Reverse Symbolism | 51 |
| 6. | Brahma's Day: The Great Cosmic Cycle and the Age of the Ṛg Veda | 59 |
| 7. | The Antiquity of the Ṛg Veda | 71 |
| 8. | A Lost Anatolian Civilization—Is It Vedic? | 77 |
| 9. | Calendric Astronomy, Astronomic Dating, and Archaeology: A New View of Antiquity and Its Science | 85 |
| 10. | Víshṇu as an Astronomical Symbol from the Vedas to the Purāṇas | 109 |
| 11. | A Date and Place for the Mahābhārata | 117 |
| 12. | Astronomy, Symbolism, and Ancient Indian Chronology: A Date for the Rāmāyaṇa | 125 |
| 13. | The Indus Civilization—An Astronomical Perspective | 131 |
| | Glossary | 137 |
| | Notes | 143 |
| | Photographs | 159 |
| | Index | 163 |

# INTRODUCTION

In the early seventies the editor of a national newspaper asked me to write one or more articles centered on the rather surprising fact that the twelve signs of the Western zodiac exactly coincide with the twelve signs of the Indian zodiac. I immediately pointed out to him that it was not as if the West had borrowed astronomy from India. Mathematics, yes. Philosophy, maybe. But as far as astronomy was concerned India's contribution had not been very remarkable—rather India had received Greco-Babylonian astronomy, for example, through contact with Greeks from the time of Alexander, around the fourth century B.C.

The disappointed editor was good enough to carry on with the idea of the articles, even though now there was no element of sensation left. Before writing the articles I wanted to cross-check the various facts about the history of Indian astronomy. To my surprise, I did not find a single cogent document on the subject. There were divergent views of diverse scholars, but no accepted body of knowledge. More than twenty years later, the position is much the same. If anything, the articles collected in this volume will make the situation much worse!

Since I had committed myself to writing the articles, however, I thought I would refer directly to some primary sources. For some strange reason—probably because of my admiration for the epic—I chose the Mahābhārata, surely an unlikely primary source for astronomy! But soon this move paid rich dividends! In the English translation there was an entire hymn on the Aśvíns quoted from the Ṛg Veda, and this hymn mentioned the twelve signs of the zodiac. That was most exciting, because the material of the Mahābhārata may not be authentic in terms of chronology; indeed some scholars have insisted that portions were added to the Mahābhārata as late as the early centuries of the Christian era.

But the Ṛg Veda was quite a different proposition. All Western scholars were unanimous that it was written prior to 1200 B.C. If zodiacal signs were mentioned in the Ṛg Veda, then they would precede Greco-Babylonian astronomy. So I raked through the Ṛg Veda to locate this particular hymn. At the same time I looked at this part of the Mahābhārata in its original Sanskrit. On both accounts I was disappointed. The hymn from the Mahābhārata had not mentioned the twelve signs of the zodiac explicitly. Nor was this hymn to be found in the Ṛg Veda itself.

In the process, however, as I combed through the hymns to the Aśvíns in the Ṛg Veda, I was totally bewildered. This whole mass of literature didn't really seem to make much sense. But suddenly, as if lit by a flash of lightning, my confusion turned to illumination.

The Ṛg Veda is considered to be a religious, philosophical, or literary document, yet the hymns to the Aśvíns were speaking pure astronomy, even modern astronomy. As for the hymn in the Mahābhārata, supposedly quoted from the Ṛg Veda, it turned out that the language and meter of this hymn is definitely Vedic—in that sense it is not a later fabrication.

That was the beginning of my study of Vedic astronomy. I did write a couple of articles for my editor friend—but the articles were very different from what I had expected. I found myself encountering a most extraordinary and interesting situation. The Vedas, and I subsequently came to realize, the Purāṇas, contain fairly advanced astronomical concepts far ahead of their time in terms of the conventional chronology, but in a highly camouflaged form. This completely upsets the rather smug history of astronomy as conceived by the scholars of the past couple of centuries.

In my opinion, the root of the problem has been the starting hypothesis that the Ṛg Veda was the composition of simple, pastoral, unsophisticated tribes. This has been further aggravated by the fact that many of the scholars who studied, translated, and interpreted the Ṛg Veda did not have a science background, in particular, they knew little astronomy.

My approach, on the other hand, had been without any preconceived notions, and my methodology had been, generally, that of modern science, namely, (1) economy of hypotheses, what is popularly referred to as Occam's razor; (2) maximal simplicity of explanations; and (3) internal consistency.

As I went on, I realized progressively that I had to free my thinking completely from the constraints of the accepted socio-historico–geographical framework.

It is possible that at times in these chapters I have overstated my case, just as at times I might have understated it. But my main thesis is based on the following conclusions:

1. Our view of prehistory and antiquity, including ancient chronology and the history of ancient science, needs to be revised.
2. The earliest Vedic period dates back to a little beyond 10,000 B.C., and the Vedic hymns contain a continuous tradition of astronomical observations right into the third millennium B.C.
3. Vedic, and even Purāṇic, literature contains a great deal of astronomy, in a deliberately obscure form. One can find in this literature both the memory of even more ancient times and also ancient astronomy itself unfolding. This astronomy is surprisingly advanced—the concepts in fact, can be compared with those of Newtonian times, and in some cases even later times. Much of this knowledge, however, was lost over the millennia because the meaning of the allegory or the "key to the code" itself was lost.
4. Once all this is recognized, a meaningful scenario can be

reconstructed out of this very obscure astronomy or astro-mythology. This could well be the key to a lost civilization, or at least to the understanding of remote antiquity. In fact, the conclusions of Giorgio de Santillana and Herthe von Dechend would be just the tip of the iceberg.[1] But this is not the task of one person, or of even one generation.

Before proceeding further I would like to digress to give a rough description of ancient Indian literature. First we have the Vedic literature, which consists of the four Vedas—namely the Ṛg Veda, Yajur Veda, Sama Veda, and the Atharva Veda—the Brāhmaṇas, the Āraṇyakas, the Upanishads, and the Vedāṅgas. The Vedāṅgas, which are six in number, are tools to understand the Vedas. Of the four Vedas, the Ṛg Veda is considered the oldest, the Atharva Veda the most recent. The other important body of ancient Indian literature we will encounter consists of the itihâsas and Purāṇas, including the epics, the Mahābhārata, the Rāmāyaṇa, and several Purāṇas. These are of later origin and could possibly contain portions added from time to time.

Indeed, the existence of rather advanced concepts like the sphericity of Earth and the cause of seasons is quite clear in Vedic literature. For example, the Aitareya Brāhmaṇa (3.44) declares: "The Sun does never set nor rise. When people think the Sun is setting (it is not so). For after having arrived at the end of the day it makes itself produce two opposite effects, making night to what is below and day to what is on the other side. . . . Having reached the end of the night, it makes itself produce two opposite effects, making day to what is below and night to what is on the other side. In fact, the Sun never sets. . . ."[2]

Similarly the following passage from the Ṡatápatha Brāhmaṇa (1.6.1–3) shows an equal insight: ". . . if even while the foremost were still ploughing and sowing those behind them were already engaged in reaping and threshing. . . ."[3]

It is in this light that statements in the Ṛg Veda (1:164) such as "Those that come hitherward they call departing, those that depart they call directed hither . . . ," are to be understood.[4]

The Purāṇas also exhibit traces of fairly advanced ideas. For example, the water cycle is quite graphically described in the Āditya Hṛídayaṁ of the Rāmāyaṇa. The Mahābhārata too expounds many modern truths. It declares (3.42.24) that though the stars appear small because of their distance, they are very large. Interestingly, the Mahābhārata speaks of an instrument that makes small things look big. It may be mentioned in this regard, that in South America concave lens-type objects have been found made of stone and dating to around 1400 B.C.[5]

So also the Víshṇu Purāṇa gives quite an accurate description of tides: "In all the oceans the water remains at all times the same in quantity and never increases or diminishes; but like the water in a caldron, which in consequence of its combination with heat, expands, so the waters of the ocean swell with the increase of the Moon. The waters, although really neither more nor less, dilate or contract as the Moon increases or wanes in the light and dark fortnights. . . ."[6]

It is quite remarkable that the Mārkaṇḍeya Purāṇa (54.12) speaks of Earth as being flattened at the poles and bulging at the equator, that is, not perfectly spherical.[7] The Víshṇu Purāṇa, in an obvious elaboration of the above quotation from the Aitareya Brāhmaṇa, also speaks of antipodes of Earth and indeed implies the existence of Earth's rotation.[8] In addition, even more elementary concepts like the phases of the Moon and the cause of twilight were well understood, as was the fact that the blue sky is nothing but scattered sunlight (cf. Mārkaṇḍeya Purāṇa, 78.8, or 103.9). One cannot gloss over all these instances, merely attributing them to later additions.

Similarly, one frequently encounters the concept of the Sun being at the center of the solar system (cf. Mārkaṇḍeya Purāṇa, 106.41). All this pales, however, before the concept, startlingly similar to the twentieth-century model, of an oscillating universe, or more accurately, a universe being cyclically created and destroyed, with just about the right time period of about 10,000 million years (cf. Mahābhārata Ṡānti Parva, or Mārkaṇḍeya Purāṇa, 81, 57–58.)[9]

Not just astronomy, but other physical concepts appear in quite a developed form in ancient Indian literature. These include atomism, superposition of various sound notes, the division of time into very small units of the order of a 100,000th of a second, and so on.

For example, the Víshṇu Purāṇa in an insightful passage declares, "How can reality be predicated of that which is subject to change, and reassumes no more of its original character? Earth is fabricated into a jar; the jar is divided into two halves; the halves are broken to pieces; the pieces become dust; the dust becomes atoms. . . ."[10]

So also, the Bṛihádāraṇyaka Upanishad (2.4.7ff.) dwells at length on the following theme, "As when a drum is beaten, one cannot distinguish its various particular notes, but they are included in the general note of the drum or in the general sound produced by different kinds of strokes. . . ."[11] Similarly, the Purāṇas define the *paramâṇu*, which is on the order of a few hundred thousandths of a second.

In addition to the physical sciences, very interesting and modern concepts of botany and biology, including the concept of micro-organisms, are also encountered in these ancient texts; for example, in the Mahābhārata,

> They [trees] drink water by their roots. They catch diseases of diverse kinds. Those diseases again are cured by different operations . . . as one can suck up water through a bent lotus stalk, trees also, with the aid of the wind, drink through their roots. They are susceptible to pleasure and pain, and grow when cut or chopped . . . they are not inanimate . . .
>
> *Vrīhí* and other so-called seeds of rice are all living organisms . . . again [men] . . . while walking about hither and thither kill innumerable creatures hidden in the ground by trampling on them; and even men of wisdom and enlightenment destroy animal life, even while sleeping or in repose themselves . . . the Earth and the air all swarm with living organisms."[12]

Much of my earlier work was concerned only with astronomy and astronomical concepts without any reference to history and chronology. But sooner or later I had to come face-to-face with these last two aspects, particularly because of the crucial role of the Ṛg Veda in clarifying the early history of the so-called Indo-Aryans, and Indo-Europeans in general. Indeed, several decades ago, the Indian scholar Bal Gangadhar Tilak and the German scholar Hermann Jacobi pioneered the astronomical dating of the Vedic period.

But the topic became confused because of the chronology of the nineteenth-century European Indologist Max Müller. His date of circa 1200 B.C. for the Ṛg Veda was at best a crude guesstimate, a date to be tentatively used in the absence of any other estimate. It, however, got concretized into a dogma and mixed up with the infamous Indo-Aryan invasion theory. This, coupled with the bias—advertent or inadvertent—of many of the European scholars of the past two centuries, has distorted the history of science and history of India, and indeed, even global prehistory. And while this point is being reconsidered in recent years,[13] it is also true that many Indian scholars have been led astray by emotion.

Toward the end of 1990 it became apparent to me that many of the astronomical references in the Ṛg Veda could be meaningfully interpreted if they were set against a date of 7300 B.C., and at first sight this appeared to me completely absurd. I had taught for many years that civilization in the true sense of the word began with Sumeria and Egypt in the fourth millennium B.C., while around 8000 B.C. the last of the great Ice Ages was still in the process of thawing. How could Ṛg Vedic civilization, with its knowledge of agriculture, astronomy, the spinning of cloth, horseback riding, and so on, be taken back to early Neolithic times? Yet the conclusion was inevitable, and I wrote about this in the paper, "Mahāyugá: The Great Cosmic Cycle and the Date of the Ṛg Veda" (now chapter 6). After its publication, I did something audacious: I started asking a few friends of mine who had an archaeological background whether there had been any recent discoveries of a civilization going back to the eighth millennium B.C. This was quite a mad thing to do, but I was convinced that civilization itself would stretch back that far. A German friend rang me up to inform me that indeed the discovery of such a civilization in Anatolia had just been announced by Professor Herald Hauptmann of Heidelberg!

This was sensational news—a long shot had paid off! I obtained the original German article and an English translation as soon as possible. This to me was the verification of a theory, in the language of modern physics. What mattered was that there was indeed a civilization with Megalithic elements going back into the eighth millennium B.C., whether it be Vedic or not.

As I started going over the photographs, I came across one that was as sensational as that civilization itself. This photograph showed a clean-shaven head with a tuft of hair hanging from the back, snake-like. Western archaeologists were hard put to interpret this sculpture, possibly the oldest sculpture known today. They described it as a skin-headed God with a snake attached to the back of its head. But even a not-too-well-informed Indian can make this out to be a sculpture of a Vedic priest, because such a hairstyle is a dying, but still alive, tradition in India today. The principle of maximal simplicity, if not astronomical chronology, would suggest that the sculpture represents a Vedic priest or something of that style, rather than the far-fetched explanation of a clean-shaven head with a snake attached at the back!

Subsequently I visited the site of the excavation at Nevali Cori in Anatolia, not because I could throw any light on it from an archaeological point of view, but only to verify for myself that the photograph of the Vedic priest's head was not misleading, as sometimes photographs can be.

I would like to make a few additional remarks about some of the articles appearing in this book:

With regard to chapter 6, I would like to draw attention to the debate on whether the northern course, the Uttarâyaṇa or Deváyâna, begins with the Sun at the winter solstice or the Sun at the vernal equinox. This is a crucial point if the chronological dating is based on this consideration alone. This is not the case with the dates proposed by me. I would like to point out, however, that all ancient sources refer to the winter solstice and not the vernal equinox, except possibly one. This is the reference in the Śatápatha Brāhmaṇa (2.1.3.1). The point has been discussed at length by B. G. Tilak in his *Orion.*[14] His opinion was that the vernal equinox was the older tradition, whereas the winter solstice is a later tradition. But the Śatápatha Brāhmaṇa is a much later text. Moreover, it would contradict the consistent scheme worked out in these chapters as well as the references in the Vedic literature. For example, the declaration that the Aśvíns open the heavens, given the arguments in this book, refers to the epoch 7300 B.C. when Aśvinī *nákshatra* was at the winter solstice. If this is interpreted to be the vernal equinox, we get an unacceptably late date for the Ṛg Veda—in the first millennium B.C. In any case, explicit references to the vernal equinox and other considerations described in some of these chapters rule out the vernal equinox as the gateway to the heavens.

With reference to the chronology of the Ṛg Veda earlier than 7300 B.C., two possible objections could arise: the absence of both spun cloth and the domesticated horse at such an early date. As the article that is chapter 9 in this book was in press, however, it was discovered that indeed cloth was being spun at that time in the Anatolian region. This fact was added as a postscript. The objection to the domesticated horse is not as serious. First, as has been noted by contemporary Indian scholar S. B. Roy,[15] the word *áśva* in very early Ṛg Vedic times could have meant a sort of an ass. Second, it is recognized as a distinct possibility that the domesticated horse was indeed present in Anatolia in the eighth millennium B.C.[16] It is even possible that the domesticated horse was present in the Mehrgarh area in the seventh millennium B.C.

With reference to chapters 5 and 10, I would like to stress the advanced astronomical and scientific concepts disguised in a profound and beautiful allegorical form. For example, consider the epithet Padmanābha of Víshṇu. The lotus, *padma,* is the Earth that springs from the navel *(nabha)* of Víshṇu the Sun, and is supported by the umbilical cord. This theme has been depicted in many beautiful sculptures over the centuries. What makes this symbolism even more profound is the fact that just as the mother nourishes the unborn infant through the umbilical cord, so also the Sun nourishes Earth that is born of the Sun.

Another thought-provoking epithet is that of Ādiśesa, the serpent that supports Víshṇu, the Sun. The serpent has already been described to be the symbol of rotation. Thus Vāsuki, the serpent coiled round Earth, describes Earth's rotation. But it is quite significant that the rotation of the Sun is described as *adi,* the first. In fact, the Sun's rotation was the original rotation in the solar system from which the planets derive their own circular and rotary motions.

With reference to the Great Cosmic Cycle referred to in chapters 6 and 9, two questions may be asked: Was the precession of the equinoxes known in such ancient times when Hipparchus supposedly discovered it around 100 B.C.? Did the ancient Indians know of the Chaldean saros or eclipse cycle, supposedly a Babylonian discovery?

In this connection the following points may be noted:

1. The Maitrī Upanishad already explicitly speaks of the Pole Star moving away.
2. As pointed out in these chapters the seventy-one years plus a fraction mentioned in the various Purāṇas is a clear giveaway, this being the period in which the equinox precesses through one degree.
3. The concept of the great *yugá* refers to a super saros, a period during which the equinoxes, nodes, planets, the Sun, and the Moon return to their original position.
4. In fact, the one-thousand–year yugá in ancient India refers to a period during which the equinox precesses through one *nákshatra.*
5. Finally, it may be pointed out that the Sūrya Siddhânta uses a far more accurate value of precession than the supposedly borrowed Greek value. Whitney, a European scholar of Indian astronomical texts, called this value of 54 seconds (of arc) a "lucky hit."

Given the elaborate context, the input of the saros cycle in computing the Mahāyugá is certainly quite reasonable.

I would also like to add a note to chapter 11 titled "A Date and Place for the Mahābhārata." It is pointed out there that a possible location for the Mahābhārata war based on the total solar eclipse of June 24, 1311 B.C., would be a place of latitude somewhat above 35 degrees in eastern parts of China (around Xixiang Province). Subsequently I learned that indeed at this very spot, and in the second millennium B.C., according to relatively new archaeological evidence, there lived an Indo-European people conjectured to be the Tocharians, the Tushāras of Mahābhārata.[17]

I would like to conclude with the following general remarks. The studies in this book appear in roughly chronological order and illustrate a two-decade-long progression of thought and discovery. To eliminate redundancy, similar articles have been combined into single chapters, but some overlap does occur, which is inevitable because in many of the articles it was necessary to recapitulate earlier results.

I felt that it was necessary to publish a collection of most of these articles, because that would facilitate an overall view and thereby a critical review. In the process, the papers have been revised and recast somewhat in features like references, and in some cases two separate articles have been combined into one chapter. (See below.)

Critical examination of these ideas would be a welcome and useful exercise, provided such an examination is free of any type of dogma and, equally important, is knowledgeable; that is, it requires of the scholar a sufficient background in astronomy and in Vedic and Purāṇic literature in particular, and all other topics involved. When the shouting dies down, it is the meek voice of truth that is heard. Ultimately, as the ancient Indian saying goes, truth alone triumphs.

The contents of this book are based on the following papers of mine:

"Glimpses of the Amazing Astronomy of the Ṛg Veda," *Indologica Taurinensia*, 4 (1978); Proceedings of the Third World Sanskrit Conference, Paris, June 20–25, 1977.

"Did Indians Pioneer Astronomy?" *Journal of Birla Planetarium*, Calcutta, 1, no. 2 (1978).

"The Heliocentric Theory in the Ṛg Veda," *Journal of Birla Planetarium*, Calcutta, 1, no. 2 (1978).

"Ancient Indian Astronomy—A Surprise," *B. M. Birla Science Centre Research Communication*, December 1985; paper presented at the International Symposium on Oriental Astronomies of the International Astronomical Union, November 1985.

"Astronomy of the Ṛg Veda," *B. M. Birla Science Centre Research Communication*, January 1988; paper presented at the International Symposium on Ancient Astronomies, 1987.

"The Unmythical Purāṇas: A Study in Reverse Symbolism," *Griffith Observer* 53, no. 4 (1989).

"The Secret Astronomy of the Hindus," *B. M. Birla Science Centre Research Communication*, January 1991.

"Brahmā's Day: The Great Cosmic Cycle and the Age of the Ṛg Veda," *Griffith Observer* 59, no. 11 (1995) (based on *B. M. Birla Science Centre Research Report*, February 1991).

"Is the Ṛg Vedic Civilization the Oldest? A Case for Rewriting History," *B. M. Birla Science Centre Research Report*, August 1991.

"The Antiquity of the Ṛg Veda," *B. M. Birla Science Centre Research Communication*, December 1991; paper presented at the International Symposium on Indian and Other Asiatic Astronomies.

"A Lost Anatolian Civilization—Is it Vedic?" *B. M. Birla Science Centre Research Communication*, December 1992.

"Calendric Astronomy, Astronomical Dating, and Archaeology: A New View of Antiquity and Its Science," *B. M. Birla Science Centre Research Communication*, July 1993; paper presented at 31st ICANAS, Hong Kong, 1993 (Chinese translation of the paper appeared in the proceedings).

"The Astronomical Symbolism of Víshṇu from the Vedas to the Purāṇas," from "Víshṇu in Art, Thought, and Literature," Birla Archaeological and Cultural Research Institute, Hyderabad, 1993.

"A Date and Place for the Mahābhārata," invited talk at the International Workshop on Application of Remote Sensing for Archaeology and Related Disciplines, National Remote Sensing Agency,

December 17–19, 1993 (in *Abstracts and Invited Talks*).

"Astronomy, Symbolism, and Ancient Indian Chronology: A Date for the Rāmāyaṇa," paper presented at the International Symposium of Ancient Indian Chronology, B. M. Birla Science Centre, Hyderabad, January 1994; Also *B. M Birla Science Centre Technical Report*, January 1994.

"The Calendric Astronomy of the Vedas," *Bulletin of the Astronomical Society of India* 26 (1998): 107–12.

"The Indus Civilization: An Astronomical Perspective," paper presented at the International Conference on Indus Civilization, Jaipur, February 1996.

"Astronomy in Ancient Indian Literature, Art, and Sculpture," paper presented at the National Symposium on Indian Astronomy Through the Ages, Hyderabad, 1997.

# 1

# The Case for Indian Astronomy

Never before has astronomy been so relevant or exciting as today. It is also the oldest science and the forerunner of modern science. What is India's contribution to it? The traditional Western view is that Indians hardly contributed to the development of astronomy at all; they merely transmitted Babylonian and Greek astronomy to the Arabs, who finally acquainted Europe with it.

But there is another possibility: the Babylonians got astronomy from India. Let us first briefly survey Babylonian and Greek astronomy.

From 2000 B.C. or earlier, the Babylonian priests were scanning and charting the sky. They had observed that rising in the east and setting in the west is common to all celestial objects. In addition, the Sun, the Moon, and the five planets then known displayed individual motions, all confined to a belt in the sky—the zodiacal belt. The planets Mercury and Venus always appeared close to the Sun. Thus, they appeared a little before sunrise in the east, as Morning Stars, or a little after sunset in the west as Evening Stars. About 700 B.C. the Babylonians compiled an astronomical text, Mul Apin. This speaks of the motion of the Moon, the Sun, and the five planets in the zodiacal belt. Little was known of the planets, though. Thirteen or fourteen star-patterns in this belt are mentioned in this text. The Babylonians did not yet divide the zodiac into the twelve signs in each of which the Sun spends one month. The earliest known text that features the zodiacal signs appears around 400 B.C. On this basis, the Romans, around 47 B.C., formulated the forerunner of our present calendar with twelve fixed months in the year. Until then a calendar with twelve lunar months and a periodic thirteenth month was used.

The Babylonians conceived of the universe as a closed box, Earth being its floor. Beyond Earth were mountains that propped up the sky. But some Babylonian astronomers probably realized that Earth is round. The astronomer Kidinnu, about 700 B.C., knew of "precession." This is a subtle effect causing the Pole Star to change its position over the course of some centuries.

The wealth of information from clay tablets reveals the Babylonian obsession with astrology. They were primarily astrologers. No wonder they hardly attempted to interpret or explain their observations.

From about 600 B.C. the Greeks became acquainted with and borrowed Babylonian astronomy. Thales, Pythagoras, and others traveled widely over Asia Minor, Egypt, and probably to India. They learned Babylonian astronomy firsthand. Later, Alexander transported piles of Babylonian clay tablets to Greek libraries.

The Greeks transformed Babylonian astronomy by studying it scientifically, that is, by trying to interpret their observations, and by theorizing. Pythagoras was the first Greek to suggest, around 550 B.C., that the Morning and Evening Stars were identical. Prior to this, the Greeks thought that Venus when appearing as the Evening Star, Hesperos, was different from Venus appearing as the Morning Star, Phosphorus. Pythagoras was also one of the first to suggest that Earth was round. About 150 B.C. Hipparchus discovered "precession," probably independently of the Babylonian Kidinnu.

By A.D. 150, over a span of five centuries, the Greeks had evolved a model of the universe with the spherical Earth at the center. The Moon, Sun, planets, and stars were attached to spheres spinning round Earth. However, a brilliant Greek, Herakleides, had suggested around 350 B.C. that Mercury and Venus revolved about the Sun, not Earth. This would explain their oscillatory type of motion about the Sun, being ever close to it. The idea was rejected.

Greek astronomy dominated the world for over 1,500 years until Copernicus, Kepler, and others laid the foundation for modern astronomy.

The early Indian contribution to astronomy has not been recognized since there is no documentary evidence. The earliest Indian astronomical text available is the Jyotisha Vedāṅga, composed as an aid to the Vedas around 1350 B.C. In this text there is no evidence of advanced or remarkable astronomical knowledge.

There is no need, however, for clay tablets or papyrus scrolls to learn about ancient Indian astronomy. We can refer to the Vedas. *Veda* in Sanskrit means "knowledge." The Vedas have been religiously transmitted, orally, across thousands of years and hundreds of generations of Brāhmins, who have blindly believed them to be the revelations of the gods. This conservatism has preserved the Vedas intact. The continuity is evident. Even today, millions of Hindus daily chant the Gāyatrī mántra of the Ṛg Veda.

The Ṛg Veda is the oldest Indian text and one of the oldest surviving in the world. This collection of hymns of sages like Vásiṣṭha, Viśvāmitra, Agástya, Dīrghátmas, and others was compiled over a span of a few hundred years. The verses of the Ṛg Veda form a code that, properly interpreted, reveals an amazing amount of astronomical knowledge, which is unbelievable when we consider their antiquity—1500 B.C. being a conservative estimate. In fact, the Ṛg Veda, shorn of its allegory and metaphorical camouflage, is the oldest textbook of modern astronomy.

A glossary of certain Ṛg Vedic terms with their proposed meanings can be compiled. Such a scheme (1) makes several unintelligible verses meaningful; (2) shows consistency, that is, makes several verses meaningful with a minimum of hypotheses, unlike present ad hoc explanations; and (3) is a natural consequence of the verses themselves.

From this approach it follows that (1) the Ṛg Vedic seers were scientists in the modern sense, having performed experiments and acquired knowledge comparable with that of recent times. Pre–Ṛg Vedic astronomers had, in fact, measured the sphericity of Earth, established the heliocentric theory in its modern form, and explained the seasons astronomically. Advanced concepts like the cause of auroral displays were also understood. (2) The Ṛg Vedic seers were inhabitants of or had visited far northern climes, up to about 80 degrees north latitude. This is Bal Gangadhar Tilak's conjecture, which is strongly vindicated on astronomical grounds. (3) The Ṛg Veda is more than five thousand years old.

Without going into the details of the code, but in the light of the above remarks, we can get glimpses of the advanced astronomy of the Ṛg Veda.

The Ṛg Veda repeatedly refers to Earth and the heavens as "bowls," thus suggesting that the sphericity of Earth was recognized. This can be confirmed from several other hymns as well.

Several hymns in the Ṛg Veda are attributed to the twin Aśvíns, but there has been some doubt as to their identity. A closer look reveals that the Aśvíns are the planets Mercury and Venus.

The twin Aśvíns are repeatedly invoked in the morning and in the evening. Mercury and Venus are seen either as "Morning Stars"—in the eastern sky before sunrise—or as "Evening Stars"—in the western sky after sunset. The Aśvíns sometimes move "by a path that leads aright" (that is, east to west) and at times "by a path that leads direct" (west to east) (Ṛg Veda 1.139.4).[1] This is exactly what happens: Mercury and Venus frequently move in the direct and retrograde sense, unlike the outer planets that have only occasional retrograde motions.

Sometimes the Aśvíns are described as "standing still" in Víshṇu's path—the zodiacal belt. All scholars accept that the Ṛg Vedic Víshṇu represents the Sun. "Standing still" is a reference to those points where Mercury and Venus appear stationary as they change their direction of motion. The Aśvíns are described as roamers or wanderers, a term used much later by the Greeks. The word *planet* is Greek for "wanderer."

Thus the Ṛg Vedic seers had recognized the identity of Mercury and Venus as Morning and Evening Stars. Moreover they had a good idea of their apparent motions, including stationary points.[2]

That the heliocentric theory was known can also be seen from the explicit statement that the Aśvíns ". . . compass round the Sun when afar . . ." (RV 1.112.13). "When afar" means those positions of Mercury and Venus when they are farther away from Earth, that is, near about superior conjunction.[3] The Ṛg Veda thus anticipates Herakleides by more than a thousand years. Furthermore, the notion that Mercury and Venus orbit the Sun was accepted only after A.D. 1500!

A Ṛg Vedic hymn refers to the twelve fixed parts of the wheel and also to the twelve forms in connection with the Sun. The hymn next describes the twelve lunar months specifically mentioning the thirteenth additional month required in this scheme. A Ṛg Vedic hymn to the Aśvíns, quoted in the Mahābhārata, also refers to the twelve zodiacal signs. Undoubtedly, the twelve zodiacal signs were known. Other hymns also support this conclusion. This is probably the origin of the later conception of the twelve Ādityas or Sun gods. In fact, the British scholar Professor Wilson, one of the nineteenth-century translators of the Ṛg Veda, in his translation of the verse 1.155.6 in a different—and incorrect—context uses the twelve zodiacal signs to explain a hymn. The earliest reference to the zodiacal signs is, therefore, in the Ṛg Veda, not in Babylonian literature.

Another Ṛg Vedic hymn has recently been interpreted as giving the value of precession (this is elaborated on in later chapters). In the Upanishads too, knowledge of precession is evident in statements like "even the fixed Pole Star deviates." The Upanishads are at least about 2,500 years old. Thus the Babylonian Kidinnu and the Greek Hipparchus were also anticipated.

It is obvious that the Ṛg Vedic seers were not mere observers in the sense the Babylonians were. They had theorized about their observations, beating the Greeks by over a thousand years in this process. They had realized that astronomical phenomena were controlled by very definite laws, a fact that is repeatedly emphasized in the Ṛg Veda. The Vedic seers, unlike the Babylonians, were primarily astronomers, not astrologers.

How did the Babylonians get astronomy from India? Through contact, both at the personal and mass level.

For instance, there is a reference to one Asurivasin at King Janaka's court at Videha. Asurivasin refers to a resident of the Assyrian city of Ashur. Then, the Persians and the Hindus belonged to the common Aryan stock. The clay tablets discovered at Boghuz Koi, near Asia Minor, in 1907, yield further confirmation of this. These are a record of a treaty between the Mitani and the Hittite tribes, around 1400 B.C. Among the deities invoked as witnesses to the treaty are the Ṛg Vedic Uruwna (Váruṇa), Índra, Mitra, and Nā̆satya (Aśvíns). The interpretation, though not unanimous, is that at this time the Aryan "invaders" were still streaming into India. It is more likely, however, that at this time at least, the flux was away from India. The reasons for this are: (1) If the Aryans invading India knew of the clay-tablet technique of writing, why is there no evidence of such tablets in India? (2) The Ṛg Veda was, in all probability, compiled before 1400 B.C. (3) The Ṛg Vedic deities are not the products of unenlightened tribal imagination or mythology, as the Boghuz Koi inscriptions imply. They are personifications of subtle astronomical and natural phenomena. History will be rewritten on this consideration. The Ṛg Vedic conception of God is highly enlightened and monotheistic. For instance, the hymn 1.164.46 declares, "One all is Lord of what is fixed and moving, that walks, that flies, this multiform creation." (4) The passage from Váruṇa, literally "all-encompassing sky" in Sanskrit, through Uruwna of the Boghuz Koi inscriptions to Ouranos or Uranus (sky) of the much later mythology of the Greeks who flourished near Asia Minor is clear. In fact, the Ṛg Veda declares, "Firm is the seat of Váruṇa," while Hesiod describes Ouranos as the firm seat of the gods.

In any case, the link between the Ṛg Vedic Indians and the peoples of the Near East is obvious.

Moreover, from 1746 B.C. to 1180 B.C., a mountain tribe, the Kassites, ruled Babylonia. During this period, astrology was developed to a great degree. Astronomy too was studied. The Kassites were Aryan. Significantly, their names bear the unmistakable Ṛg Vedic stamp, for example, Shurias, their chief god; and the Marytas (from Sūrya and the Mấruts of the Ṛg Veda); and Simalia, queen of the snowy mountains (compare with Himalāya); and so on. Through such cultural currents, the Babylonians got astronomy from India. And it is the Indians who pioneered astronomy.

# 2

# The Astronomy of the Hindus

The oldest Hindu literature consists of the four Vedas. In fact, the oldest of the four Vedas, the Ṛg Veda, is also the oldest surviving piece of Indo-European literature. The Vedas, as indeed much of the literature related to them, the Brāhmaṇas, Āraṇyakas, and Upanishads, constitute a huge body of often obscure and poorly understood hymns. To this day there is no internally consistent and coherent interpretation of the Vedas.

Meaning, however, has been forced out of the hymns—but this meaning is based on a number of socio-geographico-historical assumptions about the Aryan invasion of India. The basic outline is as follows:

The Aryan tribes were pouring into India around 1400 B.C. They were a hardy warrior race, rather simple in mind. Like all primitive people they deified natural phenomena and invoked these deities in poetic form to help them in their battles, particularly against the dark-skinned natives, the *dásyus* and *dāsas.* The body of Vedic literature consists of these hymns and their accompanying rituals.

An important piece of evidence cited in support of the above picture is the clay tablet inscriptions found at Boghuz Koi in Turkey, once the capital Hattush of the Aryan tribe, the Hittites. The clay tablets invoke the names of typical Ṛg Vedic deities, like Índra, Nā́satya (Aśvíns), Mitra, Váruṇa, and others, as witnesses to a peace treaty following a battle between the Hittites and another tribe, the Mittani.

The hymns of the Vedas themselves, however, upset this neat picture. The hymns are obscure, mysterious, and demonstrate a certain degree of artifice—not what simple tribal folk would compose. The clincher is that no consistently meaningful explanation of the hymns is available to date. The interpretations are forced and ad hoc.

For example, if, as is supposed, the Ṛg Vedic *sapta síndhu* and Sárasvatī are names for the rivers in northern India and the *dásyus* and *dāsas* the dark aborigines, how do we explain the well-accepted equivalent Avestan and Iranian river names, *hapta-hendus* and Haraquaiti, and the *dahyus* and *dahae*? This point has been glossed over by scholars. For their part, some classical Ṛg Vedic scholars like Muir and Roth have also pointed out that *dásyus* and *dāsas* hardly represent indigenous non-Aryan tribes.[1]

The Ṛg Vedic measure of gold, the *mana* (or *mina*) found in ancient Babylonian trading seals, and the old Babylonian name for Indian silk, that is, the Ṛg Vedic name Sindhu, denoting its place of origin, again upsets the picture of Indo-Aryans invading northern India around 1500 B.C.[2] In fact, on the contrary, in recent times scholars have identified the so-called "invaded" Harappan civilization with that of the so-called invading Vedic Aryans.[3]

In this context it would be good to remember the danger lurking in historical assumptions. For example, modern archaeological dating techniques reveal that the structures of Stonehenge date back to about 2800 B.C., which debunks the long-held dogma that Mesopotamia was the epicenter of civilization and that Stonehenge was built under the Mycenaean influence, sometime after 1600 B.C.[4] At an earlier epoch and in higher latitudes some form of a working civilization had already existed. The earlier date of circa 1800 B.C. for the Harappan civilization itself has been pushed back to 3000 B.C. and beyond.[5]

Furthermore, there is no archaeological or other concrete evidence to support the accepted scenario.

In addition, this picture of the Vedic Aryans being a simple, rustic lot, deifying nature and natural phenomenan in a primitive tribal fashion, immediately and blatantly contradicts the very subtle and enlightened metaphysics of Vedânta whose beginnings can already be discerned in the Vedas themselves.

Finally, the justification for the date, circa 1500 B.C. for the Ṛg Veda is based on an assumed rate of diffusion and change in language. This conclusion is at best tentative.

Given these remarks, a close but open-minded scrutiny of the Vedic hymns reveals that a very consistent interpretation with an economy of hypotheses can be obtained with a new set of assumptions. First, these hymns were composed by a highly intelligent people with a fairly advanced working knowledge of astronomy, which was enlightened enough to include concepts like precession, heliocentrism, and the sphericity of Earth, and which matches the astronomical knowledge of the seventeenth century A.D. at the very least. And second, the hymns are not religious prayers but astronomical and other scientific facts or discoveries deliberately and cleverly camouflaged. As the Ṛg Veda declares (1.164.39): "The Riks [hymns] are in the highest, undecaying heaven, wherein are situated the shining ones. What can he do with the Riks, who does not know that?"

Hymn 1.105.18 of the Ṛg Veda illustrates this point. If taken at face value, it reads, "a ruddy wolf beheld me once, as I was faring on my path. . . ." There are three crucial words here that, if interpreted differently, completely alter the meaning. These are *mā*, *sakrit,* and *vṛíka*. As they stand, they mean, "me," "once," and "wolf," respectively. According to Sayana, however, *vṛíka* here means the Moon. In fact, this was pointed out much earlier by Yaska, who realized that the word *vṛíka* was a shortened form for the Moon.

Furthermore, *māsakrit,* if the words *ma* and *sakrit* are read as one word, would mean "maker of the month." Accordingly, the same passage has the following totally different meaning: "The Moon, the maker of the months, looks at the *nákshatras* while he moves through them."[6] This is a description of the *nákshatra* or lunar calendric system, which is still in use today in the various *pañcâṅgas* or indigeneous calendars.

This example of deliberate camouflage suggests that the Vedas should be studied, not in a conventional manner, but rather in the light of Galileo's famous anagrams, for example, "The mother of love emulates the shapes of Cynthia," which means that Venus exhibits phases like the Moon.[7] It is important to note that unless this deliberate camouflage behind the hymns is taken into account, a consistent and meaningful interpretation of the Vedas may never emerge.

Some further examples of coherent astronomical interpretations are given hereafter.

## THE AŚVÍNS

A number of hymns in the Ṛg Veda are attributed to the twin Aśvíns, and their true identity has been the subject of much controversy. According to one school of thought the Aśvíns represent day and night, according to another they were demigods, and yet another holds that they were astronomers. They have also been identified with the stars Castor and Pollux of Gemini. As discussed in chapter 1, in the hymns of the Ṛg Veda the Aśvíns are repeatedly invoked in the morning and in the evening. Seen either as "Morning Stars"—in the eastern sky before sunrise—or as "Evening Stars"—in the western sky after sunset, Mercury and Venus would be likely candidates for the Aśvíns. Likewise, when the Aśvíns are described as seeking "midair by a path that leads aright [that is, east to west] as by a path that leads direct [west to east]" (RV 1.139.4), one cannot help but note that, unlike the outer planets that have only occasional retrograde motions, Mercury and Venus frequently move in the direct and retrograde sense.

"Ye as ye [Aśvíns] travel overtake the courser" (RV 1.180.2) is another telling reference. The courser here is the Sun, which is frequently referred to as such. Mercury and Venus move faster than the Sun and frequently overtake it.

The Aśvíns are also described as *chakrâvaka (cakwa)* birds (RV 2.39.3). According to legend, the male and female cakwa birds are condemned to spend the night on the opposite banks of a river. Thus the reference is to either Mercury or Venus appearing as the Evening Star in the west while the other appears as the Morning Star in the east.

The Aśvíns are said to share a common brotherhood. In fact, Mercury and Venus are the only two planets that fall into one category: they both always appear close to the Sun, in fact, are never more than 46 degrees from it. Sometimes the Aśvíns are "standing still in Viṣṇu's striding places" (RV 8.9.12). The Ṛg Vedic Víshṇu is, as all scholars accept, the Sun, and "Víshṇu's striding places" means the zodiacal belt. This is clearly a reference to the stationary points against which Mercury and Venus change their direction of motion in the zodiacal belt.

The heliocentric theory of the Aśvíns was propounded by the three Ṛibhus, the sons of Sudhanvan, who are described in the Ṛg Veda as having built a chariot for them.

## Índra, Sóma, and the Ṛibhus

Índra is the dominant deity in the Ṛg Veda and is invoked in about one-fourth of the extant hymns. A close reading of the hymns reveals that Índra is the invisible atmosphere that scatters sunlight, destroys darkness, and creates day and twilight, and that is also responsible for seasonal phenomena.[8]

In the Ṛg Veda Índra fills the midair region, holding asunder the earth and sky. He supports the sky, a reference to the fact that the sky is nothing but the scattered bluish light of the Sun.

Any number of hymns speak of Índra killing Vṛitrá with the thunderbolt of Víshṇu. Víshṇu (literally "all-pervading") is of course the Sun, whose rays are all-pervading. Vṛitrá is the demon of darkness destroyed by the sunlight that is scattered in the atmosphere.[9]

Having slayed Vṛitrá, Índra becomes invisible, or his mother hides him, and so on. This is a reference to the fact that the atmosphere is invisible. For example,

> Índra fills midair. . . .
>
> When thou hadst slain with might the dragon Vṛitrá, thou Índra didst raise the Sun in heaven for all to see. (RV 1.51)
>
> Índra with dawn, Sun and rays dispels the darkness. (RV 1.62)
>
> Índra lieth hidden. . . . (RV 6.90)
>
> [Índra] measures out the air more widely, supports the sky. . . .
>
> The terrible one of whom they ask, "Where is he," of whom they also say, "He is not. . . ." (RV 2.12)
>
> There is no Índra. Who hath beheld him? (RV 8.89)

Similarly, Índra destroys Ushas, morning twilight (RV 4.51), an allusion to twilight disappearing as daylight spreads. In particular, the seven rivers that Índra releases are the seven component colors of sunlight.

> Índra disclosed the waters and again . . . hast let loose to flow the seven rivers. (RV 1.32)

These seven colors of sunlight are also the seven steeds of the Sun:

> Constellations pass away like thieves together with their wheels before the all-beholding Sun . . . ,
>
> Seven baysteeds harnessed to thy car were thee (Sun). O thou far-seeing one. (RV 1.50)

It may be pointed out that the concept of the seven horses of the Sun, survives in India to this day. An attempt has been made to identify the seven horses with the seven days of the week, but this does not make sense because the week was never used in India. But the seven-colored rainbow is called Ịndradhanús, a term originating in the Atharva Veda, referring to the fact that the atmosphere (Índra) splits sunlight into seven components. The waters and cattle that Índra repeatedly lets loose in a number of Ṛg Vedic hymns refer to the atmosphere that scatters the rays of the Sun. As is well known, the water droplets in the atmosphere disperse sunlight, prismlike, and cause the rainbow to appear. The Mahābhārata specifically mentions that "cattle" is the secret name of rays of light.

Índra also gives the Sun in the east, a dark complexion (RV 5.33), which is an allusion to the fact that the setting or rising Sun appears orange owing to atmospheric refraction, and not, as is pointed out ad hoc by scholars, to an eclipse.

This brings us to very mysterious ground, namely, Sóma and the Ṛibhus. Sóma is solar radiation. Like Índra, Sóma has sharp weapons and a thousand-pointed shaft. "He" rides on the same car as Índra. It is bright and is offered almost exclusively to Índra. Sóma is swift. "He" is often likened to or associated with the Sun. Sóma stimulates Índra, and in fact, is his accomplice in Índra's battles to vanquish Vṛitrá. Moreover, he is the child and milk of the sky, and ". . . of him whom Brāhmaṇs truly know as Sóma, no one ever tastes" (RV 10.85).

The three Ṛibhus were the earliest astronomers, already ancient in Ṛg Vedic times. Índra is their lord. The many wonderful things that they did are described in the Vedic hymns, and these have a simple astronomical interpretation. For example, when it is said that they made a cup or chalice that was single into four cups, this refers to the fact that they had established the sphericity of Earth and that there are four distinct zones on Earth, namely, the two twilight zones, the daylight zone, and the darkness zone.

Other hymns are also clever allegory. In Ṛg Veda 1.110–11, the Ṛibhus measured with a stick to fabricate this fourfold cup and made a cow out of a skin and fashioned a calf beside it. Earth is referred to as a cow not only in Vedic but also Avestan literature, and it is significant that the Mahābhārata (3.435) gives this impoṛtant and mysterious clue—a cow beside its calf denotes Earth! Aside, then, from measuring Earth with this stick, this really means they had shown that the supposedly flat Earth is round by using a stick to perform an experiment with its shadow, similar to Eratosthenes' demonstration around 250 B.C.

Any number of other pieces automatically fall into place in the light of the preceding. For example, a revealing passage in Aitareya Brāhmaṇa (3.4.44) sheds light on the following: Índra drinks Sóma from three beakers, a reference to sunlight contained in the two twilight and the one daylight zone illuminated by the Sun. Índra always rides his pair of reddish horses, which were made for him by the Ṛibhus. This is an allusion to the daylight zone riding atop the two twilight zones.

So too, Sóma is poured in three beakers, or it has three abodes. Also, one of Índra's flanks is in the sky, the other trails below (RV 10.119). This is a reference to the two *halves of the atmosphere*, or, equivalently, the round Earth.

This is an example of how the Ṛg Vedic deities are really very definite and subtle scientific entities and not tribal or semitribal gods. Thus, as pointed out, the Ṛg Veda antedates 1400 B.C., the date of the Boghuz-koi inscriptions, which is a treaty between the Mittani and Hittites where the gods Índra, Váruṇa, Mitra, and Nāsatya (Aśvíns) are invoked as witnesses.

## THE METRICAL CODE OF THE VEDAS

The code of Vedic astronomy is not all in allegory; there is also a metrical code.[10] This deals with one of the oldest problems of astronomy, namely, the formulation of a calendar. It is well known that in the Vedic period a lunisolar calendar was in vogue, among possibly other systems. The reason why the Vedic astronomers preferred the lunar *nákshatra* system is that it is easy to observe the Moon and its positions accurately against the backdrop of the *nákshatras*, which are groups of stars used to calibrate the Moon's monthly path.[11] Ancient astronomers soon realized, however, that agricultural activity and daily life was regulated by the seasons, that is, by the Sun. This posed a fairly serious problem. While the month—more precisely, the synodic or lunar month—defined by the interval between two successive full or new moons contains about 29.5 days, so that twelve such months contain 354 days, the all-important year of the seasons, or, more precisely, the tropical year, contains about 365.25 days. This means that there is a difference of about 11.25 days between the twelve-month synodic or lunar year of the *pañcāṅga* and the tropical year, or year of the seasons. The problem is to find a convenient reconciliation of this difference.

It may be mentioned that nonagricultural societies, for example, in Arabia, have continued to use the lunar calendar to this day. In fact, their symbol of the crescent moon with a star represents this ancient tradition.

Vedic astronomers had noticed very early on that this difference builds up to a little over a month, about 33 days in fact, every three lunar or *pañcâṅga* years of 354 days each. That is, three tropical years contain one month more than three *pañcâṅga* or lunar years. So an extra month has to be added to the *pañcâṅga* years once every three years, much like the extra day added to every fourth or leap year. This extra month is called an intercalary month. This type of calendar was already in vogue during the earliest Vedic times, and is clearly mentioned in the Ṛg Veda.

It is in this context that a few of the hymns from the Vedas can be correctly interpreted, and a code embodied in the meter of the Veda itself can be detected.

A hymn mentions that Áditi returned seven of her sons to the gods and brought the eighth son, Mārtāṇḍa, to Earth for a longer time (RV 5.72). Bal Gangadhar Tilak uses this hymn to support his thesis that the earliest Vedic composers lived in higher latitudes where the Sun would not set for several days at a stretch.[12] In my opinion, while it is certainly true that the Vedic composers lived in the higher latitudes, or at least knew of the North Polar phenomenon, this particular hymn does not refer to such a polar phenomenon at all. In fact, this piece from the Ṛg Veda is susceptible to a very exact interpretation. The key to understanding this hymn can be found in some of the hymns of the Kṛishṇá Yajur Veda and the Śuklá Yajur Veda, wherein it is mentioned that the Vásus are to be associated with the Gāyatrī meter while the Rudras are to be associated with the Trísṭúb meter (see Śuklá Yajur Veda 23). What does this mean?

The eight sons of Áditi are the eight Vásus, that is, the eight years of a calendric cycle. In fact, eight lunar years of the *pañcâṅga* fall short of eight tropical years, that is, the years we use, by almost exactly three months. So three months are the remainder or *pāda* in an eight-year cycle. Now, the Gāyatrī meter has three *pādas* or lines, each containing eight syllables. So in a cycle of eight *pañcâṅga* years, if seven years do not have an extra month, the eighth year will have to be longer by three months.

What is the meaning of Rudras being associated with Trísṭúb? The Rudras are eleven, and in an eleven-year cycle of years in the *pañcâṅga*, the number of extra or intercalary months to be added is four. Now, the Trísṭúb meter has four lines of eleven syllables each. So there is an immediate parallel with the above eight Vásus and the Gāyatrī meter. In this case the Trísṭúb meter couches the fact that in every eleven years, four intercalary months are required. Furthermore, it is also mentioned in the Ṛg Veda that the gods, that is, the years, circumambulated Agní, the Sun, thrice—and then the greatness of the Rudras become apparent. This refers to the fact that in a cycle of three eleven-year periods the number of intercalary months is twelve, that is, a year itself, thus completing another cycle. In fact, this group of thrice eleven, or thirty-three, gods is very frequently mentioned in the Vedas. This thirty-three-year cycle is similar to the nineteen-year Metonic cycle attributed to the Greek astronomer Meton who lived around the fifth century B.C., more than a thousand years after the Ṛg Vedic period, in the sense that thirty-three (solar) years equal thirty-three intercalated lunar years, just as nineteen (solar) years nearly equal a whole number of lunar months. It should also be emphasized that this metrical code could be more in the nature of a mathematical scheme *à la* continued fractions (or series), rather than a practical calendrical scheme.

Thus everything fits into place like pieces of a jigsaw puzzle, once the key to the meaning of these otherwise bizarre and obscure Vedic hymns is discovered. Similarly many other of these Vedic hymns constitute a meaningful code.

## PRECESSION

There are several references strewn all over the Indian scriptures that point to an advanced and not just a working knowledge of the laws of the universe. For example, the Maitrī Upanishad refers to the deviation of the Pole Star, which clearly establishes that even around 1000 B.C. there was a long-established tradition of astronomical observation through which scholars knew of the precession of the equinoxes and the shifting of the Pole Star. This is a subtle effect missed by most ancient astronomers.

The Great Age or Kálpa or Brahma's Day is a vast period of time that reveals the enlightened vision and concept of the universe of the ancient Hindus.[13] This period of 8,640 million years can be traced to the Ṡatápatha Brāhmaṇa.[14] It is elaborated in various Purāṇas, for example, the Mahābhārata, the Mārkaṇḍeya Purāṇa, and several others. There have been various interpretations of this vast time-concept. Some Siddhântic (mathematical) astronomers of the early centuries of this era took it erroneously to be the time for a complete cycle of planetary revolution.[15] It is rather curious that the Bhagavad Gītā describes this as the period in which the material universe springs out from the unmanifested and collapses back into the unmanifested.

The Mahābhārata in fact describes the universe to be at times vast and at times contracted. The parallel with the modern theory of an oscillating universe is, to say the least, striking. According to this theory, which is very much in the running, the universe originated in a big bang that sent all matter flying out; eventually this matter will come to a halt and collapse back. Not just the idea but the concept and time-period coincidence of the Purāṇic cosmological model and the modern cosmological model according to present-day ideas is truly remarkable. The time period is between 10,000 million and 20,000 million years as against 8,640 million years quoted in the Purāṇas.

The key to understanding the meaning of the Kálpa of 4,320,000 years' duration lies in the Trípurá episode (cf. chapter 5). This is the period in which a total solar eclipse repeats itself at the same place and time of the year, when the Sun is in the same constellation, for example, Púshya. A calculation of this period requires an accurate knowledge of the precession of the equinoxes.

There is a beautiful numerical twist that is also very typical of the secret and mysterious knowledge contained in ancient Hindu scriptures. The *kálpa* is also the product of $1^1 \times 2^2 \times 3^3 \times 4^4 \times 5^5$.

Another interesting example is the perfectly accurate water-cycle model expounded in the Āditya Hṛídaya of the Rāmāyaṇa. Here it is explicitly stated that the Sun's rays cause the water in the seas to evaporate, which then condenses into clouds and pours down as rain.

The Ṛg Veda and the Yajur Veda ( Ṡuklá Yajur Veda 3) refer to spots on the Sun long before their supposed earliest observation by the Chinese, around 800 B.C. The Ṛg Veda in fact refers to the Sun as the star of the daytime, an amazing piece of insight! The knowledge that the Sun is but an ordinary star is evident, for example, in the Mahābhārata ( Ṡānti Parva).

## CONTRIBUTIONS TO SCIENTIFIC THOUGHT: ANCIENT HINDUS VS. THE GREEKS

It is generally believed that the ancient Sumerians, Babylonians, Egyptians, and Hindus observed the sky—but in a prescientific sense: there was more of religion, ritual, astrology and superstition, and mythology in their studies.[16] On the other hand, the Greeks are hailed as the founding fathers of modern science. Though they did get initial ideas and information from Asia, they transformed the study of the heavens by making it scientific, by bringing the subject from the plane of prescience to the plane of science.

Later European thought, right up to the time of Copernicus and Kepler, was influenced by and was a direct descendent of the Greek tradition. Insofar as Copernicus (circa A.D. 1500) and Kepler (circa 1600) were victims of Greek thought (that is, dogma, as in an obsession with perfect circles), it is correct to say that Greeks contributed to scientific development.

What I would like to point out, however, is that the Greek influence actually trapped astronomy in misconceptions, and as they were also ill equipped with arithmetical techniques, they hampered and retarded scientific progress for nearly two thousand years. It is only when Copernicus and Kepler shattered these misconceptions and liberated astronomy from Greek influence, less than five hundred years ago, that science in the true sense was born and scientific development began, aided by the Hindu numerals that had by then reached Europe via the Arabs. The Greeks, however, practiced a methodology of enquiry and observation, which directly led to modern science.

In contrast, ancient Hindu thought of the Vedic and Upanishadic periods was far more enlightened, free from the later Greek misconceptions and also much closer to actual scientific reality. This system of thought, however, was lost during the course of history; neither the Greeks nor the Siddhântic astronomers of the early centuries of the Christian era, for example, Ā́ryabhaṭṭa or Varāhamihira, were aware of it, nor were they influenced by it. Had this not been the case, then modern science could have begun hundreds or even thousands of years before it actually did.

To substantiate the above conclusions, let us first survey Greek astronomy and then contrast it with the earlier Vedic and Upanishadic concepts.

## Landmarks in Greek Astronomy

1. Around 600 B.C. Thales of Miletus traveled to Egypt and Babylonia. He successfully predicted the solar eclipse of May 25, 585 B.C., based on the Babylonian eclipse cycle.
2. Mercury as Morning Star in the east was considered different from Mercury as Evening Star in the west. Around 500 B.C. Pythagoras proposed they are one and the same.
3. In 550 B.C. Anaximenes proposed that Earth is at the center of the universe and is surrounded by eight transparent crystalline spheres. To each of these spheres were attached the planets, Sun, and Moon, with all the stars attached to the outermost sphere. All these spheres revolved around Earth, and the planets and stars did not fall down because they were fixed to these spheres. This model endured with slight modifications for two thousand years.
4. Around 450 B.C. Plato and his pupils floated the idea that the circle and sphere, being the most symmetrical of figures, are perfect,

and therefore, in a perfect universe, all motions are circular. Aristotle, a pupil of Plato, proposed with others an unworkable model of the universe. Aristotle's speculations on physical science had the distinction of being almost totally incorrect, for example, "heavier objects fall faster than lighter objects."

5. Anaximenes' model evolved into the model of Ptolemy by A.D. 125. The universe was perfect and changeless except in the earthly region between Earth and the Moon; so comets, which were "earthly," were actually closer than the Moon. Supernovae were ignored in Europe largely for this reason—for how could something suddenly change in the perfect heavens? Similarly, the fact that the year, month, and other cosmic constants had fractional days was a disturbing feature.
6. Hipparchus discovered precession—the slow motion of the Pole Star—around 125 B.C. The Babylonian Kidinnu, however, might have known of this a few centuries earlier.
7. Greek arithmetic and its successor Roman arithmetic was very clumsy—not at all conducive to the development of science. Numerals were represented by letters of the alphabet and the decimal system was unknown.
8. Herakleides (circa 350 B.C.) and Aristarchus (circa 280 B.C.) were two exceptions to Greek thought—they were in the Pythagorean tradition and believed that the Sun was at the center of the universe. But they had no following.

So what did the Greek universe look like? Earth was at the center, surrounded by crystal spheres; orbits were all circular; the mathematics was clumsy. All these misconceptions were shattered first by Copernicus (heliocentrism) and next by Kepler (elliptical orbits, not spheres). Then modern science began.

## Ancient Hindu Concepts in the Vedas and Upanishads

1. According to the Ṛg Veda, Earth, like the sky, is spherical, not flat.

2. The Ṛg Veda describes accurately the motions of Mercury and Venus (the Aśvíns).
3. The Ṛg Veda repeatedly asks, "How is it that though the Sun is not bound and is directed downwards, it does not fall?"—A question asked by Isaac Newton more than three thousand years later, and no one else, because the Greeks had furnished the crystal spheres to which these objects were attached!
4. Even in Ṛg Vedic times, it was known that the stars were not at the same distance from Earth (cf. chapter 3), something of which even Copernicus was not aware, and, moreover, the heliocentric theory had already been established.
5. The concept of *ṛitá* or cosmic order pervades the Ṛg Veda, but this is very different from the dogmatic Greek concept of a perfect universe, which stifled Greek astronomy. *Ṛita*, which leads to *Ṛitu* (seasons) is harmony, not chaos. As Whitehead, a great philosopher of the twentieth century, puts it, "In the first place there can be no living science unless there is a widespread instinctive conviction in the existence of the order of things, and in particular of the 'order of nature.'"
6. The precession of the equinoxes, which was supposedly discovered by Hipparchus around 125 B.C., was known several centuries earlier to the ancient Hindus.
7. Vedic literature used large numbers and employed modern decimal enumeration, compared with the primitive Greek and Roman arithmetic. The first recorded evidence of "Hindu" numerals is at least as old as the Aśokan edicts, circa 250 B.C.

All this is more to point out a lacuna in the history of science rather than to sound like a chauvinist. On the contrary, these Vedic concepts died out in the course of history. Neither Vedāṅga Jyotisha (1350 B.C.) nor the Siddhântic astronomers like Ā́ryabhaṭṭa, Varāhamihira, or Brahmaguptad were conceptually so rich. They were far better mathematicians than their contemporaries elsewhere because there was a greater continuity in the mathematical tradition of which they were a part. But interest in astronomy had died down by their time, and they shared the concepts of the Greeks, such as the spheres. Ironically too, the Pythagoreans, like Philolaus, Herakleides, and Aristarchus, had hit upon the truth in varying degrees over two thousand years before Copernicus.[17] But they had been ignored by the conventional Greek thinkers.

The progress of civilization has not always been linear. As Whitehead points out, Archimedes who lived around 225 B.C., was ahead of the European scientists of the fifteenth century.[18] Hindu mathematics, however, was transmitted to the Arabs around A.D. 750 by scholars like Kanka of Ujjain, and later the Europeans picked it up. It was now the turn of Europe to rediscover science.

# 3

# The Heliocentric Theory in the Ṛg Veda

Few ideas have been more revolutionary in history than the heliocentric theory of the solar system. Human beings took thousands of years to realize that the solid, immovable Earth was not really at the center of the universe. Philolaus of Thebes, a pupil of Pythagoras, is credited with first attributing motion to Earth around 450 B.C. His otherwise absurd theory suggested that Earth, the Sun, and other celestial bodies all revolved around a common center. Herakleides of Pontus, a pupil of Plato, speculated around 350 B.C. that the planets Mercury and Venus move around the Sun and not Earth. This explains why they seemed to be tethered to the Sun. It is probable he even suggested that Earth rotated about its axis and revolved around the Sun. According to Archimedes and Plutarch, Aristarchus of Samos conjectured around 280 B.C. that the planets revolve around the Sun. However attractive they were, none of these conceptions were accepted.

In the fifteenth century A.D. a German cardinal, Nicholas of Cusa, wondered if the Sun was not the center of it all. By 1543 Copernicus had built his model of Earth and other planets revolving around the Sun at the center. But it still took people a couple of centuries to reconcile themselves to this idea.

The heliocentric idea was well established in the Ṛg Veda a long time ago—more than a thousand years before Philolaus. The astronomy of the Ṛg Veda was incredibly ahead of its age. Scholars estimate that its hymns were writtten around 1500 B.C. But its astronomical postulates are well camouflaged. If we see through the veil of camouflage and allegory, the Ṛg Veda emerges as the oldest text on modern astronomy.

Consider the Aśvíns. They are invoked in several Ṛg Vedic hymns. It has already been pointed out that the modern names for the Aśvíns are Mercury and Venus.[1] The Ṛg Veda declares quite explicitly that the Aśvíns "compass round the Sun when afar . . . " (RV 1.112.13). "When afar" describes the configuration where Mercury and Venus are on the other side of the Sun, that is, behind it as seen from Earth.

But what can this particular line mean? "High on the forehead of the Bull one chariot wheel ye [Aśvíns] ever keep" (RV 1.30.19). The "Bull" is meant to represent Dyaus (the sky) who is described as such in the Ṛg Veda. Elsewhere the Sun is described as "the forehead of the sky" (RV 1.59.2). The "wheel" denotes an orbit or an orbital motion. The statement can thus be deciphered to mean: "The Aśvíns (Mercury and Venus) orbit the Sun." This is a good example of the deliberate obscurity in the Ṛg Veda. Noting that the Sun is elsewhere referred to as "an eye," we can discern the origin of the idea of Śiva (Digambara) "clothed by the sky" with a third eye on his forehead.

Next is the line: "Where are the three wheels of your [the Aśvíns'] triple chariot . . ." (RV 1.34.9). The "three wheels" here refer to the three circular motions Mercury and Venus exhibit: the rising and setting common to all celestial objects; the Sun's apparent annual motion that they share owing to their always being within 46 degrees of the Sun; and, lastly, their own orbital motion around the Sun.

But another hymn from the Ṛg Veda (10.106.8) explicitly states that the Aśvíns drink *Sóma* and have forms like the Moon, that is, the phases of Mercury and Venus were observed. The Mahābhārata, in fact, does refer to a telescopic device (Mahābhārata, *Śā̇nti Parva*, section 102). The significance of the disklike citings of Venus and

Mercury, and a knowledge of their phases, is clinching proof for the heliocentric theory; if Earth were at the center of the solar system, Mercury and Venus could not have exhibited phases.

The heliocentric theory had thus been spelled out. What is mentioned in the Ṛg Veda actually constitutes a major headway in setting up the heliocentric model. The following verses reveal the advanced state of knowledge of the seers (RV 1.164): "Upon this five-spoked wheel revolving ever, all living creatures rest and are dependent. Its axle, heavy laden, is not heated: the nave from ancient times remains unbroken."

The wheel upon which "all creatures rest" is the sphere of Earth itself. The five spokes denote Earth's five geographical zones: the two frigid zones, the two temperate zones, and the tropical zone. The "revolution" refers to the rotation of Earth. "Its axle heavy laden is not heated," implies that the North and South Poles, where the axis of rotation cuts Earth, remain frozen.

The rotation of Earth is mentioned by implication in another line: "Those that come hitherward they call departing, those that depart they call directed hither," which refers to the opposite phenomena visible in the two hemispheres of Earth, for example, the setting Sun for one hemisphere is the rising Sun for the other. But as people have found it hard to believe that the seers could tell so much, this line has been construed to be a description of the revolution of planets.

The following line is significant: "Who hath beheld him as he sprang into being, seen how the boneless one supports the bony?" Rendered less literally, the boneless and the bony are understood to indicate the insubstantial, or feminine, and the substantial, or masculine. That is, Nature supports the manifested or material world. On the other hand, the respected German scholar Hillebrandt surmises that "the boneless" is the Sun, and "the bony," the Moon.[2] Reason suggests that "the boneless" would indeed imply the Sun, because it is gaseous, but that "the bony" would mean Earth, because it is, in contrast, solid and rocky. The hymn says in other words, "The Sun supports Earth." Now, apart from being meaningful, interpretations should also be consistent. Can the heliocentric theory in the Ṛg Veda be deduced from other straightforward statements? Consider this verse:

> What pathway leadeth to the Gods? Who knoweth this of a truth, and who will now declare it? Seen are their lowest dwelling places only, but they are in remote and secret regions. (RV 3.54.5)

The gods (*devas*, "bright ones"), are in fact, the stars. All the stars appear to be at the same distance as if they were attached to a sphere, the celestial sphere. This is so because human vision cannot perceive their actual distances along a line of sight. Actually their distances differ widely. Scholars have interpreted the line "Seen are their lowest dwelling places only" correctly as the constellations, that is, the positions of the stars on the hemispherical sky as seen by us. But they have failed to make sense of the next line "but they are in remote and secret regions," which really refers to the fact that the actual distances of the stars are different, more distant, and in some cases unknown. The significance of the statement is that, astronomically, unless we know that Earth goes round the Sun, we cannot appreciate the fact that the stars are at differing distances. This verse means that while only the lowest dwelling places of the stars are seen, that is, while it looks like they are attached to the celestial sphere, they are actually much farther away.

How do we know this? By measurement of the actual distances of the stars. This can be done by observing what is called a parallax, which arises when we see the same star in different positions as Earth swings around the Sun. The verse itself therefore proves that the Ṛg Vedic seers knew of Earth's motion and had made very penetrating observations.

Even Copernicus had supposed, like his predecessors, that all the heavenly objects were attached to transparent material spheres so that they did not fall down. The idea of these spheres was smashed only after Kepler had introduced the notion of his elliptical orbits in

1608. The stage was then set for Newton to ask his revolutionary question: Why is it that heavenly objects do not fall down? Hence the theory of gravitation. In this context, one particular question in the Vedas is significant (RV 4.13.5): "How is it that unbound and not supported He [Sun] falleth not although directed downward?"

Did the Ṛg Vedic seers know of gravitation too?

# 4

# Astronomy in the Ṛg Veda

It has been pointed out already that the Ṛg Veda contains a considerable amount of astronomy, including a knowledge of the sphericity of Earth, the phases of the Moon, and heliocentrism, but in a deliberately camouflaged and allegorical form.

For example, Índra in the Ṛg Veda really represents Earth's atmosphere and Sóma, solar radiation. Here are further quotes from the Ṛg Veda that confirm this identification:

Sóma gives splendor to the Sun and all his forms of light (RV 9.28). Sóma is also Índra's thunderbolt (RV 9.47). In addition, Índra (the atmosphere), destroys the darkness armed with his thunderbolt, that is, the light given by Víshṇu, the Sun. Sóma also destroys darkness (RV 9.56). In one hymn (RV 9.69), Sóma is clearly identified with the beams of the Sun, while in others (see RV 9.54), the seven streams, that is, the seven rainbow colors associated with the Sun, are attributed to Sóma.

The many wonderful exploits of Índra, sometimes in conjunction with Sóma or sometimes in conjunction with the Sun, really describe the various properties of the atmosphere, for example, the scattering of the sunlight to create day and destroy darkness, the bluish appearance of the sky due to the components of sunlight being scattered, and so on. Similarly, the fact that Índra drinks Sóma in three beakers, or that Sóma sits in three places, refers to the daylight and two twilight zones of Earth. There is the rather surprising statement that Índra lengthens the day: "For him the mornings made their courses longer" (RV 8.85.1). In fact, it is well known that due to the atmospheric refraction, the length of the day is indeed increased. The same hymn refers to the seven streams, that is, the seven streams of the Sun alluded to a little earlier, being halted by Índra. This is again a reference to the seven-colored rainbow caused by atmospheric dispersion. It has also been pointed out that in the Atharva Veda the rainbow is called Índra's bow (Índradhanús).[1] Similarly, several assertions, such as that Índra is spread on all sides (RV Valakhilya 3), are meaningful in this light.

Further, Earth is frequently referred to as a bowl (see RV 3.56), or the Moon is said to shine by sunlight (see RV 9.86). Another hymn (RV 10.44) declares that Índra (the atmosphere) keeps the two bowls apart—Earth and the dome of the hemispherical sky. From such references it becomes evident that the Ṛg Vedic composers knew of the sphericity of Earth and the cause of the phases of the Moon.

The meaning of the Ṛg Vedic Aśvíns has been dealt with in detail.[2] While there has been much confusion about their identity, it was pointed out that the Aśvíns really represent the planets Mercury and Venus. It was mentioned that once this is recognized, several otherwise inexplicable passages become perfectly meaningful astronomically. In particular the Ṛg Vedic statement that the Aśvíns circle the Sun shows that a heliocentric theory, at least as far as these planets are concerned, had already been established. It was further pointed out that the allusion in another Ṛg Vedic hymn (RV 3.54) to stars being at different distances, something that can be inferred by observing annual parallax, that is, Earth's motion around the Sun, established that the heliocentric theory for the entire solar system was also known.

Something that must also be pointed out, which is clearly mentioned in several places in the Ṛg Veda itself, is that these celestial deities have deliberate double or multiple meanings, which need to be gleaned from the context. For example, Índra is also the deity of, and identified with, the *nákshatra* or lunar asterism Jyéshṭha (Antares). Similarly Sóma is identified with the Moon and the Aśvíns are the deities of, and identified with, the *nákshatra* Aśvíns (in Aries).[3]

Hymn 2.39 of the Ṛg Veda invoking the Aśvíns is rich in astronomical content. This hymn clearly states without any camouflage or allegory that the Aśvíns, that is, Mercury and Venus, have forms like the Moon, that is, exhibit various phases. This statement alone establishes the heliocentric theory for the solar system, and provides further definite evidence for the claim. This hymn also contains several clever puns, very much in the spirit of the Ṛg Veda. For example, the twin Aśvíns are compared to a pair of hooves. The word for hoof, *śaphá*, also means an eighth part. They are compared with a pair of feet. The word for feet, *pada*, also means a fourth part. They are compared with a pair of horns. The word for horn, *śṛiṅga*, also means the crescent moon. They are compared to a pair of wheels. The word for wheel, *pradhí*, also means the disk of the Moon. All these references are to the different phases of the planets Mercury and Venus! In fact, in the same hymn (RV 9.69) they are likened to a pair of hands. The word for hand, *hasta*, also represents a pair of leather bellows, which, moonlike, contract and dilate. The same hymn refers to them as a pair of earths *(kshamū)*, a very apt description astronomically. (But because it is otherwise meaningless, scholars have interpreted this as the heaven and earth.) The same hymn, and this was pointed out earlier, refers to the Aśvíns as *chakrâvaka* birds, a comparison with a very definite meaning. It refers to the two planets being on opposite sides of the Sun.[4]

Hymn 10.106 also has some astronomically meaningful, but otherwise inscrutable references. For example, the Aśvíns are described as bent *(bhujyai)* specks *(kiráṇ)* and sickle-shaped *(sṛíṇya)*. These clearly describe the crescent-like forms of Mercury and Venus, but have confounded scholars. So also have perfectly meaningful references to the Aśvíns in the same hymn as cauldrons *(gharmá)*—in fact, being close to the Sun, they are very hot—as being solid *(pajrá)* or as being partial *(áṉśa)*.

A number of other hymns in the Ṛg Veda refer to the many forms worn by the Aśvíns, that is, Mercury and Venus (see RV 1.117). In hymn 8.76 the Aśvíns are described as *gaurs*, (literally, "buffaloes"), but the word also means "moon," a perfectly meaningful comparison. The same hymn calls them *purúbhuja*, that is, "much bent," which is a good description of a crescent.

In this connection a hymn to the Aśvíns from the Ṛg Veda quoted in the Mahābhārata is of great interest. This hymn, to the best of the author's knowledge, is not to be found in the extant versions of the Ṛg Veda. But the language, meter, style, and content of this hymn leave little doubt about its authenticity. It can be traced to the Dīrghátamas collection of hymns in book 1, and there is a strong resemblance between this hymn and hymn 1.164.

In this hymn the Aśvíns are described as discs or globes *(suvṛittau)*. They are also described as *vṛittabhūya*, an otherwise inexplicable term that can be explained as "becoming rounded." They are also described as *bhuvanani*, meaning "earths" or "worlds," as above, or as envelopers of the Sun *(ashivyayantau viváshvatah)*, exactly as described earlier.

The fact that the Ṛg Vedic composers had observed the phases of Mercury and Venus leads to the surprising conclusion that they had some instrument, at the very least a polished and curved metallic vessel, without which such observations would not have been possible. Such a telescope-type instrument could also be used for determining the annual parallax referred to above. It is remarkable that the Mahābhārata indeed mentions such a device.

Another curious statement identifies the Aśvíns with the Paṅkti meter, which is octosyllabic with five *pādas* or lines. It is remarkable that there are eight conjunctions (or oppositions of the same kind) of Venus in five years yielding the eight-to-five relationship. It is also remarkable that there are, similarly, eight conjunctions of Mercury with respect to Venus, in about five "Venus years"!

A final remark about Aśvíns and their identification with the lunar asterism Aśvinī is in order. Three principal stars of this asterism and the related constellation Aries (Meshá) are easily seen. In fact, this car of the Aśvíns (built by the Ṛibhus) has three seats (RV 3.34) and is the Moon's lover (RV 8.74), that is, as is well known, it is a lunar asterism or *nákshatra*. This, on the one hand, corroborates the traditional identification of the Aśvíni *nákshatra*,[5] and on the other, it demonstrates that the *nákshatra* system did indeed originate in the Ṛg Veda, as is quite evident from other hymns (see RV 10.85) that speak of the Moon's phases vis-a-vis the *nákshatras*.

Going beyond a purely mechanical or geometrical heliocentric theory, it is recognized in a number of places in the Ṛg Veda that the Sun is but a star of the daytime sky (see RV 6.67, 7.81, 7.86, 10.88, 10.111, 10.156). The vast multiplicity of such suns is also mentioned (RV 10.88). Further it is explicitly asked, very much in the spirit of hymn 3.54, already quoted, how is it that the Sun, unattached to anything, does not fall down? Such a vital question could not be asked, even by Copernicus thousands of years later, because the Greeks and subsequent astronomers believed that all the objects in the heaven were firmly fixed to crystalline material spheres and therefore could not fall down.

Only in the seventeenth century, after Kepler had demolished the idea of spheres, could Newton ask this question and it logically led to the theory of gravitation. It is remarkable that the Ṛg Veda speaks of the Sun's force binding Earth and other heavenly objects (see RV 10.149). This is reflected in several references in later literature; for example, in the Víshṇu Sahásranāma the Sun or Víshṇu is said to support Earth.

The fact is that the Ṛg Vedic astronomical tradition was a parallel astronomy that disappeared over the centuries, probably because of the high degree of camouflage and allegory in the hymns coupled with other historical factors.

# 5

# The Unmythical Purāṇas: A Study in Reverse Symbolism

The origin of many Hindu myths lies in the Vedic literature, including the Ṛg Saṃhita (Ṛg Veda). Elsewhere, I have pointed out that a rather surprising picture of developed astronomical concepts emerges from the tangle of the Ṛg Veda hymns. This conclusion derives from arguments based on the internal consistency of the texts and on simplicity—really, an economy of hypotheses. Here is a recapitulation of the results.

1. The Vedic god Índra is Earth's atmosphere. His thunderbolt, the Vájra, is sunlight. Vṛitrá and associated demons denote darkness, while the battle between the two is the phenomenon of sunlight scattering through the atmosphere and vanquishing darkness.
2. The twin Aśvíns denote the planets Mercury and Venus. The Vedic astronomers were aware of heliocentric theory, and they were aware of the sphericity of Earth.
3. Víshṇu is the Sun, and his three steps, as extolled in the Ṛg Veda, denote the two twilight zones encompassing the daylight zone. Sóma is solar radiation, which Índra, the atmosphere, drinks in these three beakers, namely, the two twilight zones

and the daylight zone. (An alternative explanation for the three footsteps of Víshṇu identifies them as the three points where an integral number of *nákshatras*, or lunar asterisms, coincide with an integral number of *rāśis*, or zodiacal constellations. Aside from being ad hoc, this explanation supposes that the twelve zodiacal constellations had already been traced out in the era the Ṛg Veda was composed. This contradicts the belief now held by most scholars.)

The Purāṇas, too, reveal traces of advanced astronomical concepts. For example, they seem to describe an oscillating universe with a period of 8,640 million years. That figure comes surprisingly close to modern estimates of the length of a cycle in an oscillating universe.[1] Some of these vast conceptions of time are either dismissed as coincidences or are unjustifiably linked to the Hindu theory of cyclical births and rebirths.[2]

Unlike the core Vedic literature, the Purāṇas have suffered additions and alterations. In this context it may be mentioned that many of ancient India's fanciful stories about flying contraptions, deadly missiles, and so forth, have triggered a new breed of wild speculation that invokes ancient astronauts.[3]

It is true that some of the Purāṇic myths are extremely odd. For example, the legend of Triśaṅku in the Rāmāyaṇa (of Vālmīkī) informs us that Triśaṅku was transported heavenward in his mortal body. He was not, however, admitted, and so was sent plunging back to earth. In response, Triśaṅku's patron sage Viśvāmitra proceeded to create a duplicate universe with a duplicate heaven that would accommodate Triśaṅku in his mortal frame. Alarmed, the gods restrained the sage, and Triśaṅku was left dangling between heaven and earth. This myth, shorn of allegory, can be given an entirely modern interpretation. Triśaṅku was an astronaut—or even a satellite—that was launched and remained in orbit about Earth. No matter how glib and clever this may sound, it is nothing but baseless speculation.

The Purāṇas do contain allegory, however. In some passages it is transparent. For instance, the Mahābhārata refers to an old lady who spins a fabric with 360 black threads and 360 white threads while a white horse stands by. The old lady is of course time. The black and white threads are night and day, and the white horse is the Sun. Incidentally, the origin of this symbolism is in the Ṛg Veda (1.164).

Unless we recognize the fact that the Vedic hymns and the Purāṇic myths of Vedic origin are deliberate camouflage and allegory—a code, in fact—we cannot interpret them or understand their meaning. To do otherwise would lead us to the same kind of ridiculous conclusion reached by British astronomer and popularizer Patrick Moore, who wrote,

> The Vedic priests in India believed the world to be supported upon twelve massive pillars; during the hours of darkness, the Sun passed underneath, somehow managing to thread its way between the pillars without hitting them. According to the Hindus, Earth stood on the back of four elephants; the elephants in turn rested upon the back of a huge tortoise, while the tortoise itself was supported by a serpent floating in a limitless ocean. One cannot help feeling rather sorry for the serpent![4]

In fact, after the chaff is removed, the Purāṇas have a kernel that is unmythical and exhibits what may be termed a reverse symbolism. As we shall soon see, once this kernel is recognized for what it is, several seemingly absurd myths become astronomically meaningful.

In some cases it is not difficult to give such astronomical interpretations. The legend of Dáksha is a good example.

Dáksha, we know, had a number of daughters. Different Purāṇas quote different figures (see, for example, the Víshṇu Purāṇa, the Mārkaṇḍeya Purāṇa and the Vāyu Purāṇa), but from this tangle the following meaningful interpretation emerges.[5] Dáksha was either the sky or an early astronomer who had twenty-eight daughters, who were really the twenty-eight *nákshatras*, or lunar stations, that lie along the Moon's path. The Moon spends about one day in each *nákshatra*. Actually, the Moon takes just a little over twenty-seven days to go around Earth. This means one *nákshatra* had to go. In the story it happened like this. Dáksha married off one of his daughters to Śiva. Later Dáksha performed a great sacrifice to which he did not invite this daughter. The enraged Śiva then created a terrible monster, Vīrabhadra, who destroyed this sacrifice.

We shall now consider three Purāṇic myths to show how a self-consistent and astronomically meaningful picture emerges from them.

First, we consider the legend of the Vāman avatār. In this story, the god Víshṇu descends to Earth in the form of Vāman and then measures out the entire universe in three steps. As he does this, the demon Bali sinks to the dark netherworld. Clearly the origin of this myth lies in Ṛg Veda hymns extolling the wide-striding Víshṇu and his three celebrated strides. As discussed earlier, this story refers to the three regions of Earth illuminated by the Sun—the morning twilight zone, the evening twilight zone, and the daylight zone. The demons or *rākshasas* stand for darkness. So the Vāman legend reiterates the Ṛg Veda description of the three illuminated zones of Earth and lets us identify the demon Bali, who is vanquished and sent to the netherworld, as the fourth zone—the dark zone of night. It should be observed that this interpretation also explains the oft-repeated Vedic theme of the conflict between Índra and Vṛitrá.

We next consider another queer story, the legend of the churning of the ocean by the gods and the demons. The churning rod is Mount Mandara. The churning rope is the serpent Vāsuki. Because the churning rod needed a support, Víshṇu in the form of a tortoise (Kūrmá) agreed to act as the support.[6]

The battle between the gods and the demons is the battle between light and darkness. Mount Mandara is Earth. In fact, in Purāṇic literature, Mount Mandara represents the polar regions of Earth. The churning rope, Vāsuki, which is a self-coiling serpent, symbolizes the rotation of a body about its own axis. The Kūrmá, or tortoise, always stands for slow motion and here symbolizes the slow annual motion of Earth. It is necessary to point out that this slow motion is a direct consequence of the prowess of Víshṇu, or the Sun. That is, the annual motion of Earth is caused by the Sun's gravitational force upon it—a well-known fact.

We shall return to this myth soon. But before proceeding further, it should be pointed out that the apparently absurd picture of the universe that emerges from the Purāṇas—and as described earlier in the words of Patrick Moore—is perfectly meaningful. The twelve pillars that support the world are evidently the twelve months of the year, and they are specifically mentioned in the Vedic hymns. The four elephants on which Earth rests are the Dikarin, the sentinels of the four directions (see for example, the Rāmāyaṇa of Vālmikī). These elephants rest, in turn, on a tortoise and a serpent. The tortoise is Víshṇu's Kūrmá or tortoise avatar and symbolizes the fact that Earth is supported in space in its annual orbit around the Sun. Finally, the coiled serpent represents Earth's rotation. In passing, I should mention that Víshṇu, or the Sun, himself rests upon a coiled snake—the Anantá, or Ādiśesha, which represents the rotation of the Sun on its own axis.

We next come to the myth of Śiva, who in fact, embodies the immediate cosmos encompassing Earth. Let us analyze his epithets—Digambara or "sky-clad," Trilocana or "three-eyed," Nīlakaṇṭha or "blue-throated," Candramauli or "he who wears the crescent moon on his forehead," and Tripurâri or "conqueror of the three cities."

"Sky-clad" is self-explanatory in this context. Trilocana refers to the fact that Śiva has a third eye on his forehead. I have pointed out before that the forehead of the sky is the eastern sky at dawn.[7] The Sun is specifically identified as an eye in literature, starting with Ṛg Veda itself.

Next, we observe that it is the crescent moon—not the full or half moon—that Śiva wears on his forehead, that is, on the eastern sky at dawn. This crescent then is the waning crescent moon, which appears before sunrise in the eastern sky a few days before the new moon.

To understand the epithet Nīlakaṇṭha, we must refer back to the myth of the churning of the ocean. As the gods and demons churned the waters, various objects emerged from it. That means they rose into the sky. Although there is no consistent list of objects among the various Purāṇas, we can see what happened to them with an example. Take the Moon: it was captured by Śiva to be placed on his forehead. (The poison *halāhala* also emerged).

Ultimately, as sunlight arrives in the sky, it is scattered in Earth's atmosphere. Blue light is scattered more effectively and this is what gives us a blue sky. The phenomenon is symbolized by an incident in the myth of Śiva, who is the cosmos immediately surrounding Earth. When Śiva drinks the poison *halāhala*, it causes his throat—that is, the upper regions of the atmosphere—to turn blue. So we have the name Nīlakaṇṭha. Incidentally, the ambrosia or nectar that emerges is the gentle morning twilight. Now, the Aśvíns in the Ṛg Veda are, in fact, the planets Mercury and Venus, which appear at dawn (and also at dusk). Several hymns in the Ṛg Veda describe this fact by saying that the Aśvíns bring nectar—that is, the twilight—with them. Moreover, in the Ṛg Veda, the god Índra quaffs sunlight, or Sóma, in the same way that Índra quaffs ambrosia in the Purāṇas. That ambrosia was one of the products of the churning of the ocean. Finally, at the end of the churning, the Sun shines again in the sky. It may be mentioned that Śiva wears the coiled serpent around his throat, and this again refers to Earth's rotation. We also recall that the celestial Ganges streams down to Earth, first falling on Śiva's head. I have already pointed out that the celestial streams are solar radiation, and this symbolizes the entry of these streams of solar radiation into the vicinity of Earth.

Next, the twenty-eighth *nákshatra*, whose name was Satī, was the daughter of Dáksha who was married off to Śiva and not invited to the sacrifice, and this tale refers to the fact that the twenty-eighth and redundant lunar station was omitted from the set and returned to the ordinary part of the sky, that is, to Śiva.

Finally, we come to the name Tripurāri. Śiva's destruction of three cities is described, for example, in the Mátsya Purāṇa.[8] In this story, the *daitya* Maya builds three cities, one for himself and two for the *daityas* Tāraka and Vidyunmālin. One is made of gold, and another is made of silver. The Sun is compared to gold in the Purāṇic (and even in the Vedic) literature. The Moon is likened to silver in the Purāṇas. The third city is made of iron, and these three cities were located respectively in heaven, in the midheaven, and on Earth. Also, they could move about. The god Brahma ordains that these three cities can be destroyed only by Śiva and only by a single arrow shot at the very moment when these three cities are in conjunction with the constellation Púshya (in Cancer the Crab). Finally, the fateful day of the conjunction of these cities arrives, and Śiva destroys them with a single arrow. Evidently this is an allegorical reference to a total solar eclipse, when the Sun, Moon, and Earth are all aligned. With this alignment in the cosmos immediately surrounding Earth—what I have identified as Śiva—at one stroke the Sun disappears. The Moon, too, must be invisible, for it cannot be seen at new moon, which is the required phase of the Moon for a total solar eclipse. Lastly, the part of Earth from which the total eclipse is seen is plunged into darkness.

All of this strongly suggests that the Purāṇas have an unmythical component that describes natural and atmospheric phenomena through a process of reverse symbolism. This means that more advanced concepts are deliberately rendered in terms of apparently naive symbols. By this scheme, a beautiful, meaningful, and unified picture of nature emerges from diverse, unrelated, and—at first glance—bizarre myths.

One of the objections that may be raised is that all of this requires the ancients to have had knowledge of comparatively advanced concepts, including the sphericity of Earth, the rotation of Earth, the heliocentric theory, and so on. As I have shown elsewhere, however, all of these concepts are already to be found in the Ṛg Veda, which is older than the Purāṇas.

# 6

# Brahma's Day: The Great Cosmic Cycle and the Age of the Ṛg Veda

Several Indian Purāṇas—loosely, the relatively later mythological works such as the Mārkaṇḍeya, the Bhāgavata, the Mahābhārata, and others—expound the well-known large cosmic cycle of 4,320,000 years and the even larger period of 4,320,000,000 years.[1] This cycle can be easily traced to the Śatápatha Brāhmaṇa,[2] which is one of a class of earlier works called the Brāhmaṇas, and which, on the strength of its assertion that the lunar asterism Kṛíttikā, or the Pleiades, rises exactly at the east point, some have judged was compiled around 2500 B.C.[3] Interestingly, such a vast period of time is also found in the lore of the Sumerians.[4]

The exact meaning of such a vast cycle of time has puzzled scholars through the centuries. There have been a number of interpretations based on astronomical, numerological, geological, and other considerations.

Let us first see how one arrives at this large time period. According to several Purāṇas, for example, the Bhāgavata and the Mārkaṇḍeya Purāṇas, the computation's starting point is the ordinary day and night of human beings, comprising twenty-four hours. The two fortnights—the bright and dark—of the lunar month constitute the "day" and "night" of the forefathers or *pitṛís*. The tropical year, consisting of two six-month halves, namely, the "bright" half when the Sun goes from the vernal equinox (or alternately the winter solstice) to autumnal equinox (summer solstice) and the "dark" half when the Sun traverses from autumnal equinox to vernal equinox, are the "day" and "night," respectively, for the gods—that is, it is the "day" and "night" for an observer at the North Pole.

Next, the divine year, or the year of the gods, is defined: it is 360 full days of the gods, that is, 360 years. Finally 12,000 divine years, that is, 4,320,000 years, constitute a Great Age or Mahāyugá. This Great Age is divided into four subages or yugas. Their durations decrease in the ratio 4:3:2:1. Each age consists of a main period and two twilight periods. Each twilight period is one-tenth the duration of the main period. The first age is the Kṛita Yugá, which consists of 4,000 divine years, with 400 divine years before and after as twilight periods. Next comes the Tretā Yugá with a similar 3,000 divine-year main period and twilight periods of 300 years each. Then follows the Dvāpara Yugá consisting of a total of 2,400 divine years, and finally the Kali Yugá of 1,200 divine years completes the total. The total adds up to 12,000 divine years.

An especially interesting point in this system is the inclusion of the two twilight periods, one before and one after, with each equal to one-tenth of the main period. This very strongly resembles the morning and evening twilight associated with each day. Each real twilight lasts as long as the time during which the Sun is less than 18 degrees below the horizon. And 18 degrees is one-tenth of 180 degrees, or roughly the path of the Sun above the horizon. In fact, the entire sequence leading to the definition of the divine day, that is, the day at the North Pole, and the divine year of 360 divine days is reached through astronomical analogy.

There is a second relationship of interest here. A full day of twenty-four hours consists of 86,400 seconds. That means the day and night each consists of 43,200 seconds.

The Purāṇas contain many deliberately fanciful explanations of these four ages. For example, the Mahābhārata explains that each age gets shortened compared to the preceding age because of a moral decline.

What, then, is the significance of these vast time periods? Several scholars right up to the Indian astronomers of the early centuries of the Christian era believed that in a period of 4,320,000 years, all the planets, the Moon's nodes, and other celestial "objects" returned to their starting points.[5] Yet another very recent, and exotic, school of thought attributes the Great Age and its complicated ancient breakdown into subages, called *manvantaras*, to geological epochs.[6] The great French astronomer and mathematician Laplace did not write off the Great Age as mere fancy. Rather, he wrote, "Nevertheless the ancient reputation of the Indians does not permit us to doubt that they have always cultivated astronomy, and the remarkable exactness of the mean motions which they assign to the Sun and the Moon necessarily required very ancient observations."[7]

The Great Age has a very simple but camouflaged interpretation. To unravel it, we have to remember that at the end of this Great Age the god Śiva lets loose his terrible arrow of destruction from the constellation of Púshya in Cancer. In chapter 5, I discussed this particular episode, namely, the destruction by Śiva of the three cities with a single arrow from the constellation of Púshya, and there I suggested that, shorn of the deliberate camouflage and allegory, this episode refers to a total solar eclipse.

The ancient Hindus knew that an eclipse pattern repeats itself after roughly 18 years, what is popularly called the Chaldaean saros. Further, they knew of the precessional cycle, which takes about 25,800 years. In fact, as has been noted, the Maitrī Upanishad mentions in passing, in a philosophical context, that nothing in the world is permanent and that even the fixed Pole Star moves away. There is a possibility that in the earliest Vedic times, precession was known.[8] In computing the Great Age, the Mārkaṇḍeya Purāṇa invokes the factor "71 and a fraction thereof." This is an interesting clue. In fact, because of precession, the vernal equinox moves along the ecliptic by one degree in a little over seventy-one years. When we take this into account and remember that Śiva causes a total solar eclipse in the lunar asterism Púshya, or Delta Cancri, at the end of a Great Age (as, in fact, is specifically mentioned, for example, in the Mahābhārata, Vána Parva), it is easy to see that after about 4,320,000 years a total solar eclipse recurs in the same lunar asterism when the Sun is at a fixed point on the ecliptic, say, the vernal equinox. This follows from the fact that 432,000 years are almost exactly divisible by the eclipse cycle of 6585.32 days (18 years and 11.33 days, the saros). Secondly, the period of 4,320,000 years is also divisible by the precessional cycle of 25,867 years, corresponding to a precession of 50.1 arc seconds per year, a value close to today's accepted value of 50.26 arc seconds per year. It is interesting that this concept of Śiva shooting his arrow from the constellation of Púshya originates in the earliest piece of Hindu—indeed Indo-European—literature, namely, the Ṛg Veda itself.

There is also an interesting numerical twist here: 86,400,000 equals the product $1^1 \times 2^2 \times 3^3 \times 4^4 \times 5^5$! This kind of relationship is typical of the poetic and esoteric nature of ancient Hindu astronomy.

In fact, the breakdown of the Great Age into subages whose periods decrease in the ratio of 4:3:2:1 is itself a numerical pun. The matter does not end there, however. An even longer period of time is defined in the literature. This is the Kálpa, which equals one thousand Mahāyugas, that is, 4,320,000,000 years. This is also called Brahma's daytime, there being an equally long night. Brahma is the creator. The universe itself is called *brahmāṇḍa*, or the cosmic egg. There is a universal cycle that equals but a day in Brahma's life, and it lasts 8,640 million years, or two Kalpas. The concept of this cycle has been expounded in several of the Purāṇas. For example in the Bhagavad Gītā, Kṛishṇá tells Árjuna:

> All worlds from Brahma's world (the universe) are periodic, Árjuna.
>
> They, those who know the day and night, know that the day of Brahma is a thousand yugas long and a night is a thousand yugas long.

> From the unmanifested, all the manifest things spring forth on the arrival of the day (of Brahma). On the onset of night all these sink into what is called the unmanifested.
>
> Pārtha (Árjuna), this multitude of created things having existed over and over again and helplessly destroyed at the onset of night, spring forth on the onset of day.[9]

In fact, a hundred years of Brahma constitute a Mahākalpa and so on![10]

All this sounds a little like the modern theory of an oscillating universe that begins with a big bang that sends all matter flying out until the outrushing matter comes to a halt and collapses back into a tiny speck, leading to another big bang, and so on. An entire cycle according to present-day cosmological ideas could take 10,000 million to 20,000 million years. It seems incredible that the ancient Hindus could hit upon this idea thousands of years ago. Some scholars have tended to dismiss the agreement of the order of length of the cycle as a mere coincidence, with the concept itself allegedly referring to the cycle of birth and death of human souls.[11] This is manifestly not so,[12] and seems to be a very hasty conclusion. In fact, as I have pointed out in several places the physical concepts in ancient Hindu literature seem advanced.[13] These may include the heliocentric model and a very accurate knowledge of positional astronomy.

For example, the Mahābhārata declares,

> The sky thou seest above is infinite . . . it is delightful and consists of various regions. Its limits cannot be ascertained. The sun and the moon cannot see, above or below, beyond the range of their own rays. There where the rays of the sun and the moon cannot reach are shining objects which are self-luminous and which possess splendour like that of the sun or fire . . . possessed of far-famed splendour even these objects do not behold the limits of the firmament . . . this very space which the shining ones cannot measure is full of many blazing and self-luminous worlds each above the other. . . . Who is there, however, that would set

> limits to what cannot be grasped by vision and what is inaccessible? . . . When again, His [Brahma's] form is sometimes contracted and sometimes expanded, how can anyone else except one that is equal to Him be able to comprehend His limits?[14]

Interestingly, many of the concepts in Hindu literature border on concepts in modern particle physics. To give a trivial example, the last sentence in the quotation above parallels the modern concept in quantum mechanics of a relation between the sizes of the measuring agency and the measured object. Another example is the quotation from Bhagavad Gītā given earlier. It is stated there that all created things (and this includes not just matter and energy but also space), are created out of an unmanifest "background." In my opinion the question is wide open. Did the ancient Hindus hit upon conclusions that qualitatively and quantitatively parallel those of modern cosmology?

The interpretation of the Mahāyugá at the end of which Śiva or Rudrá releases his arrow from the lunar asterism Púshya, or Tishyà, gives us a vital clue for the date of the Ṛg Veda. The Ṛg Veda, the most ancient holy book of the Hindus, is the oldest surviving Indo-European text. Its age has been a puzzle from the past century, when European and Indian scholars seriously began to consider this question. Some European scholars like Max Müller and others placed the date at about 1500 B.C.[15] This conjecture was based on historical considerations, for example, the supposed influx of Aryans into the Indian subcontinent around that time, as well as theories of language diffusion, and so on.

On the other hand Tilak, Jacobi, and Ketkar interpreted conjecturally a few astronomical references and concluded that the Ṛg Veda could be as old as 5000 B.C.[16] Ketkar used a passage from Taittirīya Brāhmaṇa to infer that Bṛíhaspáti, or Jupiter, was occulting the lunar asterism Tishyà. Tilak and Jacobi cited passages from the Ṛg Veda. Both these dates have had their supporters and detractors while others have favored an intermediate date. In any case, it has come to be realized that the Ṛg Veda was certainly composed prior to 2000 B.C.[17] In fact, if we take into consideration the statement in the post–Ṛg

Vedic Ṡatápatha Brāhmaṇa that the Pleiades, or Kṛíttikā, rises at the east point, something that happened around 2500 B.C. and the reference to the Pole Star in Patāñjali's Yoga Sūtras, the Gṛhya Sūtras, the Maitrī Upanishad, and so on, and remember that Alpha Draconis was the Pole Star around 3000 B.C., the date of the Ṛg Veda could be pushed back to circa 3000 B.C.

We now come to an astronomical date for the Ṛg Veda based on the interpretation of the Mahāyugá discussed. This refers to a period in which the nodes of the Moon, a fixed point on the ecliptic, the Sun, and the Moon return to the same lunar asterism, namely, Tishyà, or equivalently Púshya, when Rudra releases his arrow. The Ṛg Veda (10.64.8), states "Kṛiṡānu (the archer), Tishyà, archers to our gathering place, and Rudra strong amid Rudras, we invoke." In fact, the lunar asterism Tishyà is traditionally considered to be arrow-shaped. As a new yugá, indeed even the new year in Indian tradition, usually begins with the Sun at the vernal equinox, this reference in the Ṛg Veda refers to an epoch when the vernal equinox was in Tishyà or Púshya. It is well known that the terminal yugá has also been called the Tishyà Yugá or Púshya Yugá, as, for example, in the Shaḍviṉṡa Brāhmaṇa, in the Kūrmá Purāṇa, and so on.[18] Tishyà in the Ṛg Veda is invoked in the same sense as Kṛíttikā in the later Ṡatápatha Brāhmaṇa. As the vernal equinox was in Púshya or Delta Cancri, around 7300 B.C., the Ṛg Veda could be as old as that date or else refers to an earlier mythical era. For completeness, however, all other possibilities should be considered. Tishyà could have been at the summer solstice. This was the case around 800 B.C., a date too late for the Ṛg Veda, even going by the most conservative estimate. The other possibility—Tishyà being at the winter solstice—gives the Ṛg Veda a date near 14,000 B.C., which is much too early to be acceptable. Tishyà at the autumnal equinox fares even worse. Further evidence for the inferred meaning of this date is found in the following statement (RV 5.54.13): "Never vanishes like Tishyà from the sky." This is a reference to the fact that the lunar asterism Tishyà, or Púshya, would not set, that is, it was circumpolar.

We may remember that Tilak argued that the Vedic seers occupied the Arctic regions, or at least visited those regions. Or they may have formulated their astronomy with respect to an observer at the North Pole. The reference given here confirms this interpretation.

It is interesting to ask why, among the thousands of circumpolar stars, would Tishyà, an inconspicuous lunar asterism, be singled out? It may be that Tishyà was special because it was located near or at the vernal equinox and because it was one of the very few stars not circumpolar in a slightly earlier epoch, but which had become circumpolar at that time, that is, around 7300 B.C.

I mentioned earlier that the concept of the Mahāyugas originates in the Ṛg Veda itself. This can be seen from the following statement (RV 10.117.8): "He with one foot hath far outrun the biped, and the two-footed catches the three-footed. Four-footed creatures come when bipeds call them, and stand and look where five are met together."

What does this as-yet-unexplained and apparently inexplicable verse mean? The key is again to be found in the Purāṇas. For example, the Kūrmá Purāṇa, (1.29.13–15) describes the 4,000-divine-year-long (including twilight periods) Kṛita Yugá as having four feet, while three feet are associated with the Tretā Yugá, two with the Dvāpara Yugá and one with the Tishyà or Kali Yugá.[19] So the verse refers to the Mahāyugá. Next, what is the meaning of "where five are met together"? Well, at the end of the Mahāyugá there is a solar eclipse, with the Sun at the vernal equinox, and the vernal equinox is in the asterism Tishyà. This is a condition that requires the alignment of the lunar asterism, the vernal equinox, the Sun, the Moon, and Earth, five in all.

It is quite remarkable that there is evidence from three totally unrelated sources, to substantiate a date for the Ṛg Veda that I have proposed above. The first comes from the Greek historian Megasthenes, who visited India in the fourth century B.C. According to him there were 153 monarchs from the very first Ikshvāku Dynasty of the original Hindus up to his time, spanning a period of 6,042 years.[20] Megasthenes himself is considered to be a reliable scholar.[21] Incidentally Megasthenes' record is close to the Purāṇic record of dynasties on the one hand, and to the list of *ṛíshis* (sages) in the Brāhmaṇas on the other hand.[22]

The second corroboration of the date comes from an unexpected source. Certain Avestan references also indicate that the vernal equinox was in the lunar asterism Tisthriya, the Avestan version of Tishyà or Púshya.[23] The close interrelationship between the Ṛg Veda and the Zend Avesta, the Zoroastrian sacred writings of ancient Persia, is well known.

A third corroboration comes again from the Greeks. Diogenes and other Greek historians put the date of the Avestan Zarathustra at about the same time.[24] It may be mentioned in this connection that a date as early as 8000 B.C. has been proposed for the Aryans themselves.[25]

Composition of portions of the Ṛg Veda as early as 7300 B.C. would imply that Vedic civilization would have extended to several centuries before 7300 B.C., because the Ṛg Veda already contains the results of a long astronomical tradition. This would take us into the last great Ice Age, which according to geophysicists, ended about ten thousand years ago. There are two apparent difficulties here.

First, any astronomical tradition is usually deemed to result from initial agricultural activity, which is dependent on the rhythm of the seasons; second, the Ṛg Veda itself gives the impression of rich and diverse flora and fauna.

Neither of these considerations are apparently reconcilable with an ice age. Moreover, until recently, it was believed that agriculture and civilization began in Egypt and Mesopotamia around or after 4000 B.C. In the 1960s, this belief was modified by the excavations at Catal Huyuk in the Anatolian region of Asiatic Turkey. A civilization flourished there as far back as 6000 B.C.[26] More recently the British archaeologist Colin Renfrew has maintained that some form of agricultural activity might have existed in the Anatolian region even before the Ice Age ended, maybe even as far back as 9500 B.C.[27] Renfrew has also pointed out, on archaeological and linguistic grounds, that there was a developed agricultural Indo-European people in the same region before 7000 B.C. This contrasts with the more commonly accepted idea that the earliest agriculture was practiced much later in Egypt.[28] Pottery from Anatolia has been traced, however, back to around 7000 B.C.[29] All this is consistent with an earlier date for the Ṛg

Veda, but more dramatic discoveries have been made.

Very recent findings have upset accepted Indian chronology in a major way. For example, the American scholars Hicks and Anderson have dated an early Hindu copper head found near Delhi and have concluded that it is as old as about 4000 B.C. This means that Aryans had already reached northern India by that time.[30] Interestingly, this could be the key to another puzzle. Evidence for a chalcolithic (copper and stone) civilization dating back to 5500 B.C. exists, but this date is much too early according to conventional chronology.[31] Some scholars have recently pushed back the date of the Indus Valley Harappan civilization to about 6000 B.C.,[32] while traces of a pre-Harappan civilization in the vicinity dating back to between 9000 B.C. and 7000 B.C. have also been reported.[33] Shortly after I proposed my unconventionally early date for the Ṛg Veda, Professor Herald Hauptmann, an archaeologist from Heidelberg, announced at the thirteenth Turkish Excavation Congress his discovery of a well-developed civilization around Nevali Cori, which is in the same Anatolian region of Turkey as Catal Huyuk.[34] These ruins date back to the eighth millennium B.C. They include a temple that is the oldest discovered so far. Professor Hauptmann believes that there are even older ruins lying buried below, that in those days the area was lush and fertile—a veritable paradise—and that there was an elite ruling class of higher clergy surrounded by ordinary tribes. It is also apparent that there was already an evolved religious system and a developed architecture, including a form of air conditioning that exploited the flowing waters of a brook. The size of the houses is also surprisingly large. The people of Nevali Cori were attentive to detail, creative, and artistic. Even the site of the settlement was chosen with consideration for inundations. The people spent their leisure time playing a plug-in type of chess game, using animal-fat-fueled stone lamps for illumination.[35]

This is consistent with Vedic civilization, including the high degree of development of the composers of the Vedas, with a long civilization and tradition already behind them and the complex and esoteric astronomy of the Ṛg Veda. There are also references to games of dice.

In looking over the photographs of the Nevali Cori excavations, I noticed a limestone head that resembles a Vedic priest, complete with a clean-shaven head, a characteristic tuft of hair, and pigtail. Taken together, archaeological and astronomical considerations may argue for a reconsideration of our ideas about the date and place associated with the deepest roots of Vedic tradition.[36]

# 7

# The Antiquity of the Ṛg Veda

In chapter 6, I pointed out that the Ṛg Veda dates back to at least 7300 B.C. when the vernal equinox was in the lunar asterism Tishyà or Delta Cancri.[1] I also pointed out that this actually implies that the Ṛg Vedic civilization would go back well beyond 7300 B.C., because the Ṛg Veda already shows traces of a long astronomical tradition behind it. In addition, recent excavations at Nevali Cori in Anatolia, Turkey, which show Ṛg Vedic influence or similarities with that tradition and which date back to the eighth millennium B.C., support this date. At the very least, the latest excavations show that settled agricultural communities and civilization, in our sense of the term, existed around that time, that is, in the supposed Ice Age itself, and did not begin, as is now believed, around 4000 B.C.

Further support for this date of 7300 B.C. and even earlier comes from an astronomical interpretation of a number of Ṛg Vedic hymns. The key to the following interpretation is the fact that the Ṛg Vedic deities are also associated, as presiding deities, with the lunar asterisms or *nákshatra*, this being a well-known tradition that dates back to Vedic literature itself.[2] In the Ṛg Veda, frequently when a deity is mentioned, it is actually the corresponding *nákshatra* that is alluded to. With this background and an observation made earlier that the Ṛg Vedic astronomy makes reference to observations made at the North Pole, several otherwise unintelligible hymns to the Aśvíns become meaningful.

## THE EPOCH 7300 B.C.

One myth concerns the Aśvíns rescuing several sages or kings who were drowning or had fallen into pits and had remained there for ten days, for example, Átri, Viśpalā, and others. In the process the blind could see and the lame could walk. An echo of this is found in the Mahābhārata too, where a sage falls into a pit and is blinded.[3] He invokes the Aśvíns with a Vedic hymn and is rescued.

All this becomes meaningful when we realize that Aśvíns are the presiding deities of the lunar asterism or *nákshatra* Aśvínī or Alpha and Beta Arietes, which was at the winter solstice around 7300 B.C. From the North Pole, around winter solstice, that is, December 21, when the Sun was in this *nákshatra*, there would be a period of total darkness (or blindness). Moreover for about ten days around December 21 the Sun would not be changing its declination, that is, it would be at a stationary point, and bereft of its annual motion, it would appear to be neither climbing up nor down; in other words, it would be seen to share diurnal motion along with all other celestial objects. In effect, it would be lame. Átri, Viṣpálā, and others are really different names for the Sun. But this is not all. As I have pointed out, the Aśvíns are really the planets Mercury and Venus.[4] Since these planets are always close to the Sun, they would appear to be rising with the Sun after the period of total darkness, that is, they would be "rescuing" it.

Further, Ketkar had used the occultation of Bṛíhaspáti, supposedly the planet Jupiter, by the asterism Tishyà or Púshya (Delta Cancri) to deduce a date of around 4500 B.C. for the Ṛg Veda.[5] Actually Ketkar, like several scholars, erroneously identified Bṛihaspáti with the planet Jupiter. In Vedic literature, Bṛihaspáti is the Sun in one of its aspects, Agní, as in fact had been noticed by earlier scholars.[6] The identification with Jupiter is only in later literature. So the reference used by

Ketkar from the Taittirīya Brāhmaṇa actually *refers to the same phenomenon,* that is, the vernal equinox at Púshya alluded to earlier, and based upon which I posed a date around 7300 B.C. for portions of the Ṛg Veda.[7]

## THE EPOCH 8500 B.C.

Once the antiquity of the Ṛg Veda beyond 7000 B.C. is recognized, several incomprehensible hymns and references in the Ṛg Veda and Vedic literature fall into place very meaningfully. For example, the list of *nákshatras* or lunar asterisms in Taittirīya Brāhmaṇa (1.5.2) starts with Kṛíttikā or the Pleiades, as the first of the divine stars, that is, the star at the winter solstice, and ends with Víśākha (Libra) as the last, that is, the star at the summer solstice (cf. Taittirīya Saṃhita, 6.5.3). Though he notices this reference, Dikshit, a respected scholar of the last century, dismisses it because it refers to a supposedly impossible date of around 8500 B.C.[8] But exactly this circumstance is exemplified in the Mahābhārata (Mārkaṇḍeya Samasya Parva), in the story of Kārttikeya. The obscure story that in the above context becomes totally clear is as follows: Índra as the deity of the asterism Róhiṇī (Aldebaran) yields his place as head of the gods to Kārttikeya or the Pleiades. This refers to the fact that originally Róhiṇī was at the winter solstice that then shifted around 8500 B.C. to the Pleiades, Kṛíttikā. In fact, in the Mahābhārata story, there is a terrible battle and Kārttikeya (literally "born of Kṛíttikā") is split asunder, the second part becoming the diametrically opposite Víśākha (in Libra), which indeed was the summer solstice in that epoch. (Víśākha literally means "split.")

That the Kārttikeya story refers to the winter solstice in the Pleiades is also borne out by another Vyāsakuṭa or Vyāsa's riddle in the Mahābhārata (except that much of the Vedic and Purāṇic literature is a riddle!). This refers to the even more obscure story of Mārkaṇḍeya, Índradyumna, the crane Sarasa, and the tortoise. Other Purāṇic stories that are otherwise fanciful can also be meaningfully explained in this light.

# THE EPOCH 10,000 B.C.

In the Ṛg Veda, Índra is repeatedly said to press down the wheel of the Sun or steal the Sun's wheel, and so on (RV 4.28.2 or RV 4.30.3). The meaning of this becomes clear the moment we realize that Índra is the presiding deity of the lunar asterism Jyéshṭha or Antares, which is also called Índra. This star was at the summer solstice around 10,000 B.C. When the Sun reaches this point, for a number of days its declination would remain practically constant, as pointed out earlier. To an observer at the North Pole, for example, it would appear that the Sun circles parallel to the horizon—as if it had only its diurnal motion, that is, as if its annual motion temporarily ceased. This would be the simple meaning of all those otherwise mysterious statements, and a number of related hymns when taken together become clear.

In fact, the much commented upon and enigmatic story of Prajāpati and Róhiṇī originating in the Ṛg Veda (*maṇḍalas* 1 and 10) and elaborated upon in the Brāhmaṇas, for example, the Taittirīya Brāhmaṇa (1.1.10) and the Aitareya Brāhmaṇa (13.9) refers precisely to this; it alludes to Prajāpati, the year, as beginning at the winter solstice when the star Róhiṇī was at the winter solstice, at the same time that Jyéshṭha or Antares was at the summer solstice, that is, around 10,000 B.C. Furthermore, the allusion in the Taittirīya Brāhmaṇa (3.1.2) to Ajá-ékapada rising in the east, again refers to exactly this circumstance. Ajá-ékapada or the *nákshatra* Pūrva Bhādrapada, was at the autumnal equinox at the same time, that is, around 10,000 B.C., and as such would rise exactly at the east point. (Interestingly, in our times it is at the vernal equinox.)

Finally, the well-known reference to Agha or Magha (Regulus) and the Phalgunis in the Ṛg Veda again can be meaningfully interpreted as the long polar twilight occurring when the Sun was in the asterism Magha, followed by the polar sunrise when the Sun was at the vernal equinox in the asterism Phalgunīs (in Leo), in an epoch slightly earlier than 10,000 B.C.

## CONCLUSION

The connection of Índra (though taken in the classic sense of an Aryan god) with the winter solstice has been noticed by other scholars also.[9] It may also be pointed out that very recently, following a totally different route, Abhyankar, a professor of astronomy, has concluded that in Vedic times the vernal equinox was at Alpha and Beta Arietes (Aśvinī), which again yields the date 7300 B.C.[10]

In any case, two recent findings debunk the classic view that the Vedas were composed by invading Aryan tribes around 1500 B.C. First, on the basis of extensive marine archaeological research, S. R. Rao has located Kṛishṇá's city of Dvāraka—which dates back to 1400 B.C. and beyond.[11] This points to a very much earlier origin for the Vedas, which predate the Mahābhārata by a long stretch. And much the same conclusion is drawn by Hicks and Anderson, who have dated an old Hindu copper head to 3500 B.C. or beyond, and have concluded that the Aryans were already established in India around that time.[12]

All this would seem to contradict certain currently accepted notions. For example, in the Ṛg Veda there is an already established horseback riding tradition, which allegedly originated around 1500 B.C. But researchers Anthony, Telegin, and Brown have recently pointed out, on the basis of the analysis of horse teeth from the Ukraine, that horseback riding in the Ukraine dates back to 4000 B.C.[13] This again points to the fact that contemporary assumptions about Vedic civilization need to be reviewed. What I have tried to show is that there was a continuous astronomical Ṛg Vedic tradition starting from before 10,000 B.C. and extending to 7300 B.C. and later.

I would like to conclude on a purely speculative note. Recent excavations in Anatolia reveal a developed civilization going back to the eighth millennium B.C. and beyond. As such, there could certainly have been an astronomical culture at that time without any contradiction. The question is, is there any reference to, if not evidence for, a civilization dating back to around 10,000 B.C.?

Indeed, there is such a reference—Plato's account of the lost continent of Atlantis! The coincidence of the date of the hypothetical Atlantis and the proposed earliest known period of the Ṛg Vedic civilization is remarkable. Were the two linked together?

# 8

# A Lost Anatolian Civilization—Is It Vedic?

About a couple hours' drive away from Sanli Urfa, in the Anatolian region of Turkey, buried away in the almost deserted hills and valleys, is Nevali Cori, a place hardly heard of even in its own vicinity, much less visited.

Yet, at this spot a lost civilization has been excavated by archaeologists headed by Professor Herald Hauptmann of Heidelberg. The adjoining areas are rich in Neolithic or New Stone Age settlements, dating back to about 6000 B.C.; but the Nevali Cori site dates back to beyond 7000 B.C. It is a great tragedy that the oldest known civilization had, by mid 1992 when I visited the site, been all but submerged under the waters of the Ataturk Dam. However, many of the excavated materials and objects have been transported to the Archaeological Museum at Urfa.

This latest excavation is unique in that it exhibits traces of an advanced civilization. There are Megalithic features, including what is probably a temple—the oldest of its kind in history.[1] A far cry from contemporaneous primitive Neolithic civilizations, at this site there are massive structures erected in straight lines and at right angles, rather like suburban villas with stone blocks. One of the houses was sixteen meters long and seven meters wide. There was also an early form of air conditioning in each of the buildings, achieved through gaps under the floor through which water from the Kantara Stream could be made to flow. An external wall surrounds the temple, with stone plates serving as benches. Vertical pillars project from between the plates. There is a perfectly square room in the temple with a terrazzo floor of limestone chips mixed with mortar and carefully polished. In the words of Hauptmann (cf. ref. 1), "For the first time there was an attempt to form, to shape something here. The people of Nevali Cori wanted to give expression to their creative power to amuse and entertain themselves and others with new forms."

Two pillars were found in the vacant room of the temple. One of them was still in situ, where it had been erected more than nine thousand years ago. The other had been overturned and broken by vandals. These slender monoliths are each three meters high and probably supported a ceiling covering the inner yard of the temple. The pillars could be stylized human forms. The outlines of human hands going round them and meeting each other can still be clearly made out. According to Hauptmann (cf. ref. 1), "We cannot explain the pillars and the temple with our knowledge of the world."

The site at Nevali Cori appears to have been chosen with great care. It is situated about 500 meters above sea level and about 70 meters above the valley floor of the Euphrates, which made the settlement safe from the periodic flooding of the river.

This is the oldest excavated site with a layout. On one side of the temple a staircase led up to the terrazzo floor and exactly opposite, between the chiselled pillars, was located a niche in which stood the bust of what the archaeologists have concluded is the earliest depiction of God.

According to Hauptmann, this area had over nine thousand years ago been a paradise in which humans had been in harmony with the environment and had been both dynamic and creative. Archaeologists believe that the temple of Nevali Cori is not the only one at this site, but that there is another and even older one located exactly under it. This is substantiated by the fact that a part of its masonry can be seen.

This was left in place by the builders of a later era, as a protective wall against landslips. According to Hauptmann (cf. ref. 1), "It was a thing of genius to just simply put the new temple into the wall of the old one."

At this site a number of large limestone sculptures have been found, the oldest known in the world. One of them is the head of the "god" that has baffled all the archaeologists. It is clean shaven with a snakelike pigtail at the back. In addition there is a beautiful sculpture of a pelican-like bird, a bust of a young woman with a ponytail, and a few others as well. Clearly, the inhabitants of this civilization were an artistic lot.

This single excavation promises to unsettle the conventional view of history in a major way. For, according to current ideas, around 7000 B.C. or earlier, Earth was in the final phase of the last of the great ice ages; people were nomadic and pre-agricultural, and settled civilization was nonexistent. The Nevali Cori excavations blatantly contradict this theory. (In recent years, however, the view has been expressed that around 10,000 B.C., or earlier, the climate began to warm again, helped by the stabilization of sea levels.)

The inhabitants used lamps, with probably animal fat as fuel, and they even played a plug-in type of game resembling chess. There are also a number of cylindical wells, built of stone, probably used for the storage of grain, similar to those found in a number of areas right up to the Indus Valley, though of a much later period.[2] Was this a study cum meditation center, a proto-Nalanda? (Nalanda in Bihar, India, is the oldest known "university" complex in the world.)

In any case this settlement is far ahead of other contemporaneous Neolithic cultures. In fact, one conclusion reached by archaeologists is that the settlements belonged to an elite Anatolian clergy. The identity of this elite Anatolian civilization has proved baffling. I have suggested that the Ṛg Vedic civilization dates back to beyond 7000 B.C., that its earliest stages go back to around 10,000 B.C., and that the Nevali Cori civilization could be identified with the Ṛg Vedic civilization.[3] Subsequently, a remote antiquity for the Ṛg Veda of about

6000 B.C. to 7000 B.C. has been suggested independently by the American author Frawley and Abhyankar.[4] It is also remarkable that the possibility of a very early and primitive Indo-European civilization in the same area—though not Vedic, which is supposedly more advanced and later—was suggested by Renfrew.[5] In fact, recent work by, among others, Soviet archaeologists Merpert and Muchaev show agrarian settlements in the vicinity around the seventh millennium. This area has the Ṛg Vedic name Sindshar![6]

An earlier date for the Ṛg Veda of course goes against the generally accepted date of about 2000 B.C. But many of the arguments for a later date of composition are based on inconsistent interpretations of the Ṛg Veda itself, as well as certain increasingly debatable historical assumptions, for example, that the Ṛg Veda was composed by Indo-Aryan tribes invading India around 1500 B.C., and also on the basis of glottochronology. In fact, recent glottochronology itself has come into doubt, because of its assumptions.[7] As the European scholar Winternitz summed it up: "The available evidence merely proves that the Vedic period extends from an unknown past, say X, to 500 B.C., none of the evidence to the dates 1200–500 B.C., and 2000–500 B.C., which are usually assumed, being justified by facts."[8]

Even if the time frame of the Ṛg Vedic civilization agrees with the Nevali Cori civilization, this, while suggestive, is not conclusive evidence that the two are the same or were closely interlinked. A number of other considerations, however, strongly point to this linkage:

1. Probably the most impressive evidence is the sculpture of the skin-headed god that has puzzled the archaeologists. It is identical to the head of a Vedic priest, common in India even today! (see illustration). The sculpture represents a clean-shaven head with the typical Vedic braid or *śikhā*. It is also well known that the *śikhā* tradition has been extant from Vedic times, and the Taittirīya Saṃhita explicitly refers to it. So do the Atharva Veda and the Yajur Veda. It is also described in diverse post-Vedic texts like the Āśvalāyana Gṛihya Sūtras, the

Gautamá Dhárma Sūtras, in Āyurvedic texts and Purāṇas like the Brahmavaivarta and the Brahmâṇḍa.[9] It may be remarked that Egyptian and Sumerian priests also had tonsured heads, but without the typical Vedic *śíkhā* depicted in the Nevali Cori sculpture. So, the oldest known sculpture in the world may be that of a Vedic priest!

2. The archaeological evidence for a temple being built upon a temple at Nevali Cori has its immediate echo in the continuing Hindu tradition of building a temple on the ruins of an earlier temple.
3. The Nevali Cori site, as pointed out by archaeologists, quite evidently belongs to an elite Anatolian priestly class. This again fits in very well with the continuing tradition of exclusivity of the Brāhmaṇic Vedic priests and seers who composed and transmitted the Vedic literature.
4. A general description of the Nevali Cori site as it was in its heyday, consisting of an idyllic grassland with the precursors of barley and wheat—which are still present in the region—growing there, forests of oak, elm, pistachio, and other trees, and herds of wild sheep, cattle, pigs, goats, and gazelles, and temperate climate fits in remarkably well with the descriptions that can be gleaned from the Ṛg Veda. In fact, it has been observed that the flora and fauna described in the Ṛg Veda rule out many countries and territories, including India and other traditional candidates for the Vedic homeland.[10]

A possible difficulty for such an early Vedic date is the reference to horses in the Ṛg Veda. It may be pointed out that bones of wild horses have been found in this Anatolian area, dating back to long before this epoch of the Nevali Cori civilization, while recently the date of domesticated horses has been pushed back to at least circa 4000 B.C.[11]

It is well known that from at least around 2000 B.C., this very region of Anatolia had a great amount of Vedic or Indo-Aryan influence, whether it be Kikkuli's text of horseback riding with Sanskrit terms, or the Boghuz Koi inscriptions with the names of Vedic deities, or in the language and lore of many of the Indo-Aryan tribes who inhabited this and nearby areas.[12] There are also a number of similarities between the Vedic and Sumerian traditions of about 3000 B.C. For example, the typical luni-solar calendar with its intercalation or addition of extra months, or the vast periods of past history such as 4,320,000 years, or allusion to the seven sages, and so on.[13] These similarities are much too precise to be mere coincidences. A parallel of the Hindu caste system also existed in the Indo-European or Indo-Aryan cultures.

Today this and the adjoining areas in countries like Iraq and Syria are homeland to the Kurds. It is quite remarkable in the context of what has been said earlier, that the Kurds, unlike other inhabitants of this land, are Indo-Europeans. The Kurdish language, like Persian or Kashmiri, is Indo-European. For example, their word for water is *aap,* which is pure Sanskrit, as is *pur* for town, and so on. In fact, the names in a place like Urfa even today are purely Sanskritic, or even Vedic; for example, Tugra (which could possibly have been the Vedic name for Tigris), Ambar, and so on.

According to Kurdish lore, the Kurds have been in this land for several thousands of years and were originally Zoroastrians. There is justification for this claim, at least from about 2000 B.C. onward,[14] whether it be the Avestan motifs of the bronzes of Luristan, or the Avestan and Vedic influences on the language and culture of the Kassites, the Hurrites, the Hittites, the Medes, and others, not to mention the Sumerian similarities alluded to above. (Another curious similarity pointed out recently by Parpola is between the ancient Hindu *vipatha* chariot drawn by a horse and a mule and an identical Hittite custom!)[15] It may be mentioned here that, according to recent thinking, Vedic influences were transmitted to these cultures from India rather than the other way around, as previously supposed.

It is also well known that the Avesta of the Zoroastrians and the Ṛg Veda are close to the point of being almost identical at places. The

Avesta was also independently given a very old age of about 7000 B.C. by the ancient Greeks and other scholars. It is quite remarkable that certain Avestan references clearly mention that the sage Gautamá Nodhás of Ṛg Vedic fame had met with and debated a Zoroastrian personality.[16]

A strong case can be made for the Nevali Cori civilization being Vedic or very close to it.

# 9

# Calendric Astronomy, Astronomic Dating, and Archaeology: A New View of Antiquity and Its Science

According to generally accepted ideas, civilization and science began in Egypt and Sumeria in the third or fourth millennium B.C. and spread in various directions.[1] In the context of the Indian subcontinent (that is, South Asia), it is believed that Indo-Aryans, an Indo-European people, invaded the northwestern parts of the country somewhere around 1500 B.C., overrunning in the process the then existing Indus Valley or Harappan civilization.[2] The Indo-Aryans, so the theory goes, were a seminomadic, hardy, rustic, and illiterate lot who could overcome the civilized and settled Harappan inhabitants, destroying their dwellings in the process, because of their superior strength and equestrian skill.

This scenario is based on an interpretation of the earliest extant Indo-European text, the Ṛg Veda. The Ṛg Vedic hymns are supposed to be invocations to various tribal or naturalistic deities for their aid in the Aryans' battles to conquer the original inhabitants.

Recently this view has been severely criticized, for various reasons, and today is considered questionable. I would like to point out that the Ṛg Veda and the related Vedic literature, on the contrary, contain amazingly accurate and sophisticated calendric astronomy. This fact points to not an illiterate, seminomadic tribal society, but rather a well settled agrarian and meticulously scholarly people. Once the astronomical content of Vedic literature is recognized, several dates begin to emerge that blatantly contradict the prevailing picture of prehistory. It will then be shown that very recent archaeological excavations spanning a period of nearly six thousand years, from about 7500 B.C. to about 1500 B.C., can be meaningfully understood against this background.

## THE CALENDRIC ASTRONOMY OF THE VEDAS

The Ṛg Veda repeatedly emphasizes *ṛitá* or cosmic order, embodied in the periodicity of astronomical phenomena; the word for seasons, *ṛitú*, derives from *ṛitá*. Both a solar and a lunar calendar were used, with an intercalation to reconcile the two. Thus, the wheel of time has 12 parts and 360 spokes or days or 720 pairs of day-nights, with a remainder of about 5 days (RV 1.164). This is evidently a solar calendar. Interestingly, the Egyptians had a 360-day year followed by a 5-day gap.

From time immemorial Vedic Indians have been using a luni-solar calendar. The origin of this calendar is again to be found in the Ṛg Veda. Thus Váruṇa, (literally, "the all-encompassing") knows the 12 moons (that is, the twelve, 29.5-day months of a normal lunar year of 354 days). He also knows the moon of "later birth" (that is, the thirteenth intercalated month, added periodically to reconcile the lunar year of 354 days with the solar year of about 365 days [RV 1.25]). The Sumerians also used such a luni-solar calendar.

I mention this just to give an inkling of the problem at hand. A primitive society cannot be expected to calculate the year or the lunar month or other astronomical periodicities to any great degree of accuracy. The real problem of the calendar is the following: the Moon is, to quote the Ṛg Veda, the maker of the month. Thus the interval between two successive full moons, called the synodic month (or roughly, the month), is 29.5306 days (more technically, mean solar days). But the time taken by the Moon for one complete revolution about Earth, called the sidereal month, is 27.3217 days. Finally the year that we use, called the tropical year, that is, the year of the seasons, is 365.2422 mean solar days.[3]

The problem now is to devise a convenient calendar that avoids the fractional days and also the fact that twelve months do not exactly fit the year.

I would like to stress at this point that any society meticulous in its astronomical observation would choose the Moon quite naturally as a calibrator for observation because the movement of the Moon in the sky can be marked quite accurately against the background of the stars, something that is not true for the Sun. So in the earliest Vedic period, the path of the Moon was measured by twenty-seven stars or star groups. These are the twenty-seven *nákshatras* or lunar asterisms. The Moon would spend one day in each *nákshatra*. But since the Moon takes 27.3 days for a complete circuit, at an early point in time a twenty-eighth *nákshatra* was also considered. These *nákshatras* were the daughters of the sky who were wooed by the Moon. Some of these *nákshatras* are explicitly mentioned in the Ṛg Veda, while the Yajur Vedas and the Atharva Veda name them in detail. The Ṛg Veda (10.85) says, "Sóma [the Moon] in the midst of all these *nákshatras* hath his place . . . the Moon is that which shapes the years. . . . Sóma [the Moon] was he who wooed the maid [*nákshatra*]. . . ."

The *nákshatra* system endured for a very long time and is seen clearly in the astronomical text Jyotisha Vedāṅga, (circa1350 B.C.). It is in use in India even today. It was also in use in China and in the Arab world. Thus the Chinese used the twenty-eight *nákshatra* zodiac called the *shiu*, an improvement on the twenty-three *nákshatra* scheme of about 850 B.C. of the Yuehling. Some decades ago there was an unnecessary debate on the origin of the *nákshatra* system.[4]

As can be clearly shown, its roots go back to the Vedas. An important piece of evidence is the Weber manuscript, an antique document discovered around 1890 at Kugiar near Yarkand in Sinkiang Province. It describes the twenty-eight *nákshatras* of the Atharva Veda as expounded by an Indian scholar Pushkarasárdi, in the archaic

Gupta script.[5] Recently it was widely reported that an old star map on wooden blocks was salvaged from a pagoda.[6] It measures 25 centimeters by 21.2 centimeters and has been dated at A.D. 1005, making it China's oldest star map. It antedates by about one hundred years a previous star chart that was discovered in 1971 in a tomb at Xuan Hua, in northern China. The new find depicts the twenty-eight *nákshatras* in a Sanskrit incantation. (A recently discovered tomb painting from about 25 B.C., in Xian, appears to depict the twenty-eight *nákshatras (hiu)*, while the earliest mention of their names might be traced back to about 433 B.C.) The lunar *nákshatra* system could also be the symbolism behind the Arabic crescent moon and star.

The Sun, however, cannot be ignored because the year is a barometer of the seasons that regulate agriculture and all of life. Hence the need to reconcile the lunar months with the solar year.

A further remark is that in Vedic literature, the *devas*, or gods (literally, "bright ones"), denote daytime, or the bright lunar fortnight, or the northern course of the Sun, that is, from the winter solstice to summer solstice. The *asuras* (or demons), literally those prohibited from the celestial draft (of brightness), denote the night, or the dark fortnight, or the southern half of the Sun's annual course. The Ṡatápatha Brāhmaṇa (2.1.4.9) declares that the gods are indeed the day.[7]

Finally, not only are Vedic astronomical computations incredibly accurate, but they also show a way with numbers that borders on the mystic and magical, as will be appreciated below.

The Ṛg Veda (RV 3.9.9) says that 3,339 *devas* worship Agní (the Sun), who is "lord of the seasons" (RV 10.21). A simple way to understand this is that in the basic Vedic unit of 33 years there are 371 intercalary days, so that in a 9-times-33, that is, 297-year period, the number of intercalary days is 3,339. Furthermore, these 3,339 intercalary days equal almost exactly 113 synodic months. All this means that in 297 lunar years of 354 days each, 3,339 intercalary days or 113 synodic months have to be added to get back 297 solar years. So if a year starts with a full or new moon, after the 297-year cycle, the year would again start with a full or new moon. The length of the year by this calculation is an amazing 365.2424 days.

This number has a further significance; 3,339 synodic months themselves equal 270 years, a multiple of the number of *nákshatras.*

Finally, this number has a third significance, which is expressed in the very ancient Nivíds (Vaiśvadevanivid) where it says there are 33 gods, then 303 gods, and then 3,003 gods, suggesting a sort of series development.[8] We can show that this is indeed so. The 33-year unit in the Ṛg Veda has an even more basic unit, namely, 11. Thus the *devas* or bright ones or years are 3 x 11 in the earliest Vedic literature. All this can be explained as follows; in a cycle of 11 lunar years, one has to intercalate 120 days, or 4 months, to bring the period approximately in tune with tropical (ordinary) years. So in a 33-year period one has to intercalate 1 full year. Let us call these intercalated years the first-generation years. The above means that 33 first-generation years equal 33 (solar) years. In this approximation, the year is almost 365 days.

Now, consider the Vedic group of 11 first-generation years. To 303 such groups, 37 intercalary months have to be added to bring these years into tune with ordinary (solar) years. In other words, 303 first-generation 11-year groups approximate 303 eleven-year periods even more closely. The length of the year is then an incredible 365.2421 days. We can continue in this vein and at the next step, 3,003 second-generation 101-year groups would almost exactly equal 3,003 x 101 years. Thus we see the emergence of the series 33; 303; 3,003; . . . as a method of approximating the year even more closely through intercalated lunar years. This process can be continued, and is at the root of the concept of the 30 million gods of Hindu mythology.

We next come to the concept of Gandharvas in the Ṛg Veda and Vedic literature in general, a concept that has been to date grossly misunderstood. The Gandharvas are associated with the Moon or Sóma. Indeed, they observe all forms (or phases) of the Moon. According to the Aitareya Brāhmaṇa (5.27), Sóma (the Moon) lived among the Gandharvas, who returned the Moon in exchange for a woman (that is, a *nákshatra*).

Their number is given variously as 27 and 6,333. All this is perfectly and exactly meaningful if we realize that the Gandharvas represent synodic months. First, 27 synodic months (from full moon to full moon) approximately equal two years, whereas 6,333 synodic months equal 512 years very accurately. This last relation in fact gives the value of the synodic month as 29.5285 days and the year as 365.2422 days, revealing an incredible degree of accuracy.

Further, 6,333 synodic months equal 6,854 sidereal months. This means that if a year began with the full moon in a particular *nákshatra* or lunar asterism, after 512 years, the year will again begin with the full moon in the same lunar asterism.

There is a further twist: 512 is equal to $8^3$ and the well-known Gāyatrī meter of the Ṛg Veda is an 8/3 meter. The Ṛg Veda declares that the Gāyatrī meter has different functions. I pointed out one of them in chapter 2 in the discussion of the metrical code of the Vedas: In an 8-year period, there are 3 intercalary months.

Another characteristic of the meter is in the above relation of there being $8^3$, or 512, years in 6,333 synodic months. It can now be seen why, in the Ṛg Veda, the Gandharva is called Viśvā́vasu or the universal Vásu, the term Vásu being associated with the number eight. It is specifically stated that the Vásus are associated with the Gāyatrī meter.

In chapter 6, I elaborated the step-by-step build-up of days, months, and years to the cycle or Mahāyugá in Vedic literature of 4,320,000 years. This Mahāyugá or Megacycle is half a cycle and encompasses the eclipse saros and the precessional cycle as well. As I pointed out, there are 86,400 seconds in a day and, furthermore, 4,320,000 equals $1^1 \times 2^2 \times 3^3 \times 4^4 \times 5^5$. All this is to elucidate my remark about the mystic way with numbers that the Vedic composers had, in addition to their amazing degree of accuracy in astronomical observations and insight into astronomy itself. (It can be seen that the Babylonian eclipse saros and the Greek Metonic cycle are not only included in the above scheme, but far surpassed. In fact, the Māṇḍūkya Upanishad specifies the 19/7 relationship of the Metonic cycle.)[9] It is in this context that we can understand the statement in the Jaiminīya Brāhmaṇa, "Prajāpati [the lord of the *devas* or the bright halves, explained above] defeated Mṛtyu [the lord of the *asuras*, the dark halves, explained above] by numerical equivalence."

It is quite evident that the composers of Vedic literature were a highly intelligent, knowledgeable, and sophisticated lot with a long tradition of astronomy that itself implies observation and settlement. Apart from their incredible calendric accuracy, including knowledge of precession, such other advanced and modern concepts as the heliocentric theory are already evident in the Ṛg Veda itself. All of this is a far cry from what can be expected of the seminomadic, illiterate invaders that contemporary theory supposes. On this score alone, modern theories of Aryan invasion based on the usual interpretation of the Ṛg Veda and Vedic literature become totally untenable. It is not surprising therefore that in recent times emerging evidence has steadily eroded this theory.[10]

Once the astronomical and calendric character of Vedic literature is recognized, any number of astronomical dates tumble out. All of them show a continuous astronomical tradition beginning before 10,000 B.C. Many of these dates are couched in the typical allegorical style of Vedic and other ancient Indian literature. But there are a number of explicit dates also. A few are given below.

The Taittirīya Brāhmaṇa (3.1.2) refers to Ajá-ékapada, the *nákshatra* Purva Bhádrapada, rising exactly due east, a phenomenon that occurred around 10,000 B.C. when this asterism was at the autumnal equinox.

Another explicit reference is from the Taittirīya Saṃhita (6.5.3), which explicitly puts the asterism Kṛ́ttikā, or the Pleiades, at the winter solstice, an event that took place around 8500 B.C. While this was noticed by Dikshit in the past century, it was dismissed as being an impossibly old date.[11]

The Aitareya Brāhmaṇa, which is one of the earliest of the Brāhmaṇas or expository texts in the Vedas, explicitly refers to the asterism Púnarvasu (Castor and Pollux), presided over by the deity Áditi, also being exactly due east. This happened around 6000 B.C., and was noticed by Tilak, but for different reasons.[12]

The Śatápatha Brāhmaṇa, one of the latest Brāhmaṇas, refers to the asterism Kṛíttikā (the Pleiades) rising due east, which immediately yields the date of about 2300 B.C. Thus an amazing continuity of astronomy from about 10,000 B.C. to about 2500 B.C. can be seen in Vedic literature.

All this is in blatant contradiction to contemporary theories that the Ṛg Veda was composed around 1500 B.C. by the invading Indo-Aryans (who displaced the settled and civilized inhabitants of the Harappan civilization). One could ask what is the evidence for either the above date of the Ṛg Veda or the invasion theory? Surprising as it might seem, there is in fact practically no evidence, archaeological or textual to support this claim.[13] As will be seen, there is far more positive archaeological, textual, and other evidence pointing to a very old date for the Vedic civilization.

## RECENT GEOPHYSICAL AND ARCHAEOLOGICAL FINDINGS

At the time the history of antiquity was formulated, and until quite recently, it was believed that about 10,000 years ago Earth was under the grip of the last great Ice Age, which enforced a nomadic lifestyle on people. Civilization in the modern sense of the word began only after this Ice Age started thawing, which in turn made agriculture and a settled lifestyle possible. This led to the great river-valley civilizations in Egypt and Sumeria.

Recent geophysical studies of the stabilization of sea levels indicate, however, that even around 10,000 B.C. several parts of Earth had already warmed up to the extent of making agriculture perfectly feasible.[14] In fact, in recent years it has been realized that the epipaleolithic civilization of about 10,000 B.C. and earlier in and around Anatolia (Turkey) already showed traces of agriculture (the growing of grain), domestication of animals (such as goats and sheep), and permanent settlements in round houses with arrangements for storage of food. This itself was preceded by settlements with seasonal camps, dating from about 14,000 B.C.[15]

The most dramatic archaeological finding of recent times has been the relatively unknown excavatons at Nevali Cori in Anatolia.[16] This site dates back to around 7500 B.C. Current excavations there reveal even older underlying structures, showing an even older—at least several centuries older—civilization. While there are other settlements not too far away that go back to around 10,000 B.C., or earlier, the Nevali Cori civilization is unique in that it represents an already developed civilization with Megalithic elements and meticulous architecture and planning. The inhabitants were also a very artistic lot and several beautiful limestone sculptures have been found. In fact, this archaeological site contradicts straightaway the theory that civilization began in Egypt and Sumeria around 3000 B.C.

The very remarkable feature of Nevali Cori is that in civilizational terms it is an isolated oasis within the framework of present-day knowledge. It does not relate to any civilization or culture of its period. There is a gap of some five thousand years before we come to a similar civilization. With one exception.

Its echoes can be found again in the fairly recent excavations at Mehrgarh in the Baluchistan area of the Indian subcontinent.[17] The Mehrgarh civilization dates back to between 7000 B.C. and 6000 B.C. and parallels Nevali Cori in terms of economy, agriculture, domestication of animals, and the planning and layout of large settlements (Professor Hauptmann, the excavator of Nevali Cori, subscribes to this view).

The buildings at Mehrgarh were constructed of mud bricks. Several rooms were used for habitation and storage of food. Stone tools were used for harvesting cereal grasses. Ornaments were also being made. Social differentiation was also evident. By 5000 B.C., mud-brick storage houses were built and public architecture began to appear, as did handicrafts, including handmade pottery. Copper metallurgy was also present. Soon barley and wheat were also being extensively used. It is believed that between 5000 and 4000 B.C. the Mehrgarh civilization expanded. Many mud-brick storage buildings were built and now pottery was made using potter's wheels. There was a continuation in the making of ornaments and metallurgical activities. A few contemporary sites in Baluchistan and the Northwest Frontier province also appeared in this period. An article of pottery here from the period 4000 B.C. to 3500 B.C. shows the svastika symbol in a circle.

From about 3500 B.C. the Mehrgarh civilizational influence began to spread, particularly in pottery technology and styles, linking not only Central Asia (southern Turkmenistan), including the southern parts of Afghanistan and eastern Iran, but also the Harappan civilization. Stamp seals began to appear. In fact, the various interactions in the region are believed to have set the stage for the emergence of the Harappan civilization that, until quite recently, was supposed to have had a sudden and independent origin in full bloom!

The Harappan civilization is much too well known to be elaborated upon here.[18] It existed from about 2500 B.C. to about 1800 B.C. based on carbon dates (or from 3100 B.C. to 1900 B.C. with MASCA correction). Nearly one thousand Harappan sites have been unearthed spanning a vast area of 1.5 million square kilometers, from the borders of Iran, to Turkmenistan (Altyn Depe), and from northern Afghanistan (Shortughai in the Bactrian Plain), through Punjab and Gujarat right up to Delhi and the Godavari Valley. It is now believed that this civilization developed from the early Indus Valley groups, especially Kotdiji, which itself was influenced by Mehrgarh. This vast civilization displays a remarkable uniformity mirroring the settlement patterns of the towns of Mohenjodaro and Harappa.

It is now clear that fire worship was prevalent in this civilization.[19] Brick altars for fire worship were built in many houses, and in Kalibangan a row of seven fire altars was found, while one of the Harappan seals depicts worship of the fire god with seven attendants. A few seals showing a horned deity in yogic posture amidst animals have been interpreted, probably correctly, as depicting the god Śiva in his aspect of Paśúpáti, lord of animals.

There does not appear to have been a major capital or center for this vast civilization, quite unlike other ancient civilizations. This suggests what has been described as a complex chiefdom, or a series of chiefdoms strung together, rather than a unified state.

The very developed public architecture of the Harappan civilization is well known, as are the thousands of seals. The decipherment of the script of these seals has been a problem. It was believed to have been a form of an early Dravidian language, but it now appears that the language of the seals was what the Indian archaeologist Rao calls an old Indo-Aryan, more plainly, a form of Sanskrit.[20]

The Harappans had much contact with several places in Iran, Tajikistan, Bahrain, and elsewhere, as is evidenced by the Harappan pottery, weights, and seals found in those places.

It was believed that the Harappan civilization suddenly fell or disappeared. It now appears that many Harappan sites were affected by floods and by rivers changing their courses, and this led to the abandonment of settlements, in spite of the many low, protective walls built against such an eventuality. Though Harappan civilization declined, it continued in a decadent form in Gujarat and other parts of India. This phase is being labeled as the late Harappan period. Such late sites are found as far south as the present-day Maharashtra and as far east as Delhi. They extend up to the late second millennium B.C., and at these sites the painted grayware pottery of the early Iron Age is also found, indicating a direct cultural link between the Bronze and Iron Ages in the Indian subcontinent. This belies an earlier theorized Dark Age. The once-popular theory that the inhabitants of the Harappan civilization fled due to invasion is now called into question.

Around 2000 B.C. the cemeteries and tombs of the Mehrgarh region show some new features that are also found in the late Harappan civilization. These new traits are similar to those of Tepe Hissar III near Iran and Namazga V of southern Turkmenistan, and also to regions in Afghanistan like Dashly III. It has now come to light that around 2000 B.C. a vast region extending from the Gurgan Plains near the Caspian Sea (for example, Tepe Hissar) through southern Turkmenistan (Namazga, Altyn Depe), the Murghab Delta (ancient Margiana, Togolok, and so on), and ancient Bactria, including north Afghanistan (Dashly) right up to Mehrgarh in Baluchistan show uniform cultural traits. Parpola calls this the Bronze Age of "Greater Iran" or Namazga V culture.[21] It is characterized by distinctive monumental architecture, cult objects, iconographic motifs, bronze swords, and so on. Links with the Harappan civilization are also evident.

Further, the large quantity of weapons and evidence of chariots indicate the presence of a military elite—an Aryan military elite, as is generally agreed. At Dashly III a fire temple has come to light (circa 2000 B.C.) that has three concentric circular walls, and there is evidence of another such temple as well. At Togolok 21 another fire temple has been unearthed (circa 1800 B.C.). Apart from the fire altars, at the Togolok temple the ancient Vedic Sóma ritual was also practiced; the oblations were put in a row of vessels placed on special brick platforms. Further, at this site thirty miniature stone columns were discovered, as have been found at many other sites of Greater Iran. These are supposed to provide the link between the phallic cults of West Asia and the Hindu liṅga cult also in evidence in the Harappan civilization.

Apart from all these recent and comparatively recent developments, the existence of Aryan tribes in and around Anatolia—the Mittani, the Hittites, the Kassites, and so on, who lived around the middle of the second millennium B.C.—has been known for a long time. Thus the Vedic deities Índra, Mitra, Váruṇa, and Nā́satya are invoked in the Boghuz Koi (near Istanbul) oath inscriptions between the Mittani king Sati Vaja and the Hittite king Supliluliuma.[22] In addition, the prevalence of other Vedic deities like the Mā́rutas, Sūrya, and also the horse-racing terms in Kikkuli's manuscript all show a distinct Vedic and Sanskritic (Indo-Aryan) influence. There have been a number of theories about these civilizations of antiquity (but not of the newly discovered Nevali Cori civilization).

With regard to the Nevali Cori civilization, as I have pointed out, in addition to a remarkable coincidence of dates, from several points of view there is very good reason to identify the Nevali Cori civilization with the Vedic.[23]

With regard to the Harappan civilization, there has been a theory popular among European scholars for several decades, namely, the

Harappans were originally some sort of Dravidians and that around 1500 B.C., invading Indo-Aryans, who were also the composers of the Ṛg Veda, overran the Dravidian Harappan civilization and the Harappans were driven to the southern parts of India. For some of the following reasons, this theory has been called into question.

1. As mentioned earlier, the decipherement of the language of the Indus seals by Rao and independently by Kak of Louisiana and others show them to be of Sanskrit origin and not Dravidian.
2. The fire altars and the Śiva (Paśúpáti) motifs also point to a Vedic influence.
3. According to current interpretations, the forts that the alleged Vedic Aryan invaders encountered were circular, while the Indus layouts are all rectangular.
4. Rao's marine archaeological finds at Dvāraka have unearthed the lost city of Dvāraka, capital of the kingdom of Kṛishṇá of Mahābhārata fame.[24] These finds, which show a continuation of the Harappan civilization, are dated to around 1500 B.C. This date pleasingly fits a number of dates proposed for the Mahābhārata war from different viewpoints.[25] It may be pointed out that in the Mahābhārata itself the gradual submergence of the city of Dvāraka is explicitly mentioned.[26]
5. Excavations at the Harappan cemetery H show a few new features discussed above but no evidence of any intrusions of the ethnic type that could even be connected with migrations from the west.
6. The analysis of skeletal remains in southern India indicates the same Mediterranean or Caucasian types, which debunks the Dravidian theory.[27]

As the American scholar Shaffer puts it, "Current archaeological data do not support the existence of an Indo-Aryan or European invasion into South Asia at any time in the pre- or protohistoric period. . . . The Indo-Aryan invasion as an academic concept of eighteenth and nineteenth century Europe reflected the cultural milieu of that period. Linguistic data were used to validate the concept that in turn was used to interpret archaeological and anthropological data."[28]

In support of the above, I would also like to point out the following:

1. The Ṛg Vedic hymns on which current theories have been built are in fact not well understood and contemporary interpretations remain obscure and inconsistent.
2. If, as is supposed, the Ṛg Vedic Saptasíndhu and Sárasvatī are names of rivers in northern India and the *dásyus* and *dāsas* the dark aborigines, how do we explain the well-accepted equivalent Avestan and Iranian river names Hapta-hendus and Haraquaiti and the *dáhyus* and *dahae?* This point has been glossed over by scholars.
3. Some classical Ṛg Vedic scholars like Muir and Roth have also pointed out that *dásyus* and *dāsas* hardly represent indigenous non-Aryan tribes.
4. The Ṛg Vedic measure of gold, the mina found in ancient Babylonian trading seals, and the old Babylonian name for Indian silk, namely, the Ṛg Vedic name *síndhu,* denoting its place of origin, again upsets the picture of Indo-Aryans invading northern India around 1500 B.C.
5. The picture of the Vedic Aryans being a seminomadic pastoral lot deifying nature and natural phenomena in a primitive tribal fashion, immediately and blatantly contradicts not just the very meticulous astronomy outlined above but also the very subtle and the highly enlightened metaphysics of the Upanishads whose beginnings can already be seen in the Vedas.
6. The presence of the svastika signs in Indus seals is another giveaway. This has been an auspicious Hindu symbol mentioned in epics like the Rāmāyaṇa and the Mahābhārata.
7. Similarly, the presence of the pipal leaves in the Indus seals is very suggestive. This holy tree is mentioned even in the Ṛg Veda.
8. Finally, the chronology does not match the Vedic dates indicated

earlier.[29] A few scholars, however, still tend to keep the Aryan invasion theory alive by using very exotic and even inconsistent twists.

For example, in his scholarly paper the European scholar Parpola argues that the native *dāsas* and *dásyus* who were invaded by the Ṛg Vedic Aryans were probably the original inhabitants of parts of Greater Iran.[30] It is through this link that the Vedic influence symbolized in the famous Mittani-Hittite tablets of Boghuz Koi and other Sanskrit names are explained. According to this reconstruction, however, the invaders belonged to an earlier wave of what Parpola calls the Sauma Aryans, so called because they had only the Sóma ritual, with fire worship and deities like Váruṇa being the *dāsa* concepts. Further, the Sauma Aryans are identified with the Andronovo nomadic tribes of southern Russia who are dated to around 1700 B.C. The west and central Asian Aryan influences are then a fusion of the original Aryan Sóma cult and the fire cult of the *dāsas*. This latter is symbolized by the fire temple at Dashly III in Bactria, which displays three concentric circular walls. There is evidence for other circular *dāsa* forts, which were supposedly attacked by the invaders. On the other hand, the sóma cum fire altar of Togolok 21 would represent a fusion of the Aryan and *dāsa* civilizations.

The second wave of Aryans, the composers of the Ṛg Veda, is then invoked, who some centuries later streamed straight down through Afghanistan rather than turning westward as did the earlier wave. There are two difficulties with this scenario aside from the fact that no archaeological evidence exists for the destruction of the forts, which Parpola himself recognizes. If the Mittani-Hittite Aryans of Anatolia, who also lived around 1700 B.C., were influenced by the Andronovo nomads of southern Russia, the time frame becomes almost impossible. And then to top it off, there appear no traces of the Andronovo nomads in the Mittani-Hittite civilization.

There are several other places where this type of a theory becomes wafer-thin. First, the Vedic *dāsas* and *dásyus* and *asuras* were the symbols of darkness like the night, the dark half of the month, and the southern half of the year, rather than human prototypes. The circular forts of these *dásyus* or *asuras* were cosmic. The three circular forts (Trípurá) in particular, as I have argued, were Earth, the midheaven and the heaven.[31] This is clearly spelled out in the Aitareya Brāhmaṇa. These forts were also described as moving, and the *dāsas* themselves were scaling up to heaven.

Next, the fire cult is one of the oldest Vedic concepts, again with cosmic and astronomical overtones as described earlier. Furthermore, the supposedly *dāsa* deity Váruṇa has a Sanskrit name as do other *dāsas.* Also in the earliest portions of the Ṛg Veda the term *asura* is used for other Vedic deities as well. Váruṇa is the guardian of the cosmic law referred to earlier, which manifests itself in the near exact magical coincidences of the astronomical cycles that have been described.

In a sense, all of this is irrelevant to the theme of this paper, because Parpola finally concludes that the conquered *dásyus* of Greater Iran were therefore themselves Aryans.

I would like, however, to close this discussion with two other observations. The above two-wave Aryan theory, which shifts the encounters of the Indo-Aryans from Harappa to Bactria, implies that the actual conquerers of the non-Aryan *dāsas* treated the *asuras* and *dāsas* as similar to themselves, while the later Aryans treated the now Aryan *dāsas* as the conquered enemies. Finally, if fire worship was a characteristic of the original inhabitants of Greater Iran, it is remarkable that it was also characteristic of the supposedly different Harappan civilization, including far-off Kalibangan.

With this general scenario we can now discern a number of links, which form a suggestive mosaic:

1. The svastika symbol in Mehrgarh pottery, which appears somewhat later on some Indus seals, is an auspicious symbol in Indian epic literature. In addition, the Mehrgarh civilization dates back to the seventh millennium B.C. and has aspects of similarity with the Nevali Cori civilization.

2. There seems to be a connection between the fire altars in Turkmenistan (Togolok) and Afghanistan (Dashly) and the Harappan civilization, particularly Kalibangan, where there are seven fire altars, and also with the Harappan seal showing worship at a fire altar with seven accompanying deities.

   The concept of the seven fires is purely astronomical and originates in the Ṛg Veda. It is connected with the myth of the stars of the Pleiades or Kṛíttikā and the seven stars of the Great Bear or Sapta Ṛíshi (the Seven Sages), and is exemplified in the Mahābhārata. To understand this myth one has to notice that of the seven visible stars in the Great Bear, only one has a companion. There are six easily visible stars in the Pleiades. According to the myth, the fire god (that is, the Sun) was enamoured of the seven wives of the seven sages. Another maiden (Svā́hā) was enamoured of the fire god. So Svā́hā successfully took the form of the wives of the sages, that is, the Great Bear, and cohabited with the Sun. Except that the wife of one of the seven sages was so chaste that Svā́hā just could not take her form. The six wives were promptly banished. In any case the resulting semen was put at one place—this is the Pleiades, which according to the dates proposed above was at the winter solstice in early Vedic times. To conclude the myth, the result of the cohabitation was the Hindu deity Kārttikeya, who was split asunder, the second portion being the lunar asterism Víśākha, that is, one who has been split. (As pointed out elsewhere, the lunar asterism Víśākha is 180 degrees away and would have been at the summer solstice in the Vedic epoch.) Kārttikeya, born of the Pleiades, rides a peacock, probably a symbol for the several stars that constitute this lunar asterism. He is nurtured by the seven mothers. To make the identification of the Indus seal script complete, Rao's decipherment shows that the fire altar on the seals was called *gahpahppat*, which clearly denotes *gārhapatya*, the Vedic fire altar to be kept at home.

What would be the significance of the Sun in the form of a fire god, the Pleiades, and the seven sages and seven mothers for the Harappan civilization fire altar? That at the time of the Harappan civilization the Pleiades was at the vernal equinox, as in fact is explicitly mentioned by the latest of the Brāhmaṇas, the Śatápatha Brāhmaṇa.

It is quite remarkable that the peacock and stars are prominent motifs on the pottery found in the late Harappan cemetery H which pottery already shows new stylistic influences.[32] Among the objects found there was an urn or pot with seven seedlike objects in it that can be directly compared with the above myth. So while the styles may have changed, the concepts seem to show a continuity.

The seven sages and seven mothers and seven seeds have an exact parallel in the Zoroastrian Haptaoring (in Sanskrit *saptaliṅga* or the seven phallic objects), and the seven sages of Sumerian lore. There is an equal parallel with the seven deities of the Hittites. In fact, the parallel is made closer if we observe that in the Hittite custom a goat approaches the deities. In the Pleiades myth from the Mahābhārata related above, a goat is also present. The link with the Hittites is of course quite natural. Apart from the many other known parallels, recently Parpola has pointed out another curious similarity between a chariot drawn by a horse and a mule in Hittite custom and the identical ancient Hindu *vipatha* chariot. Also, a few Hittite invocations are practically in Sanskrit. For example, the Hittite "Istanue Ishami," compares exactly with the Sanskrit, "Sthānu Is'ami."[33]

Similarly, from very early on a deity seated in yogic pose amid animals depicted on Harappan seals has been identified with the Hindu Śiva. This again throws up a contradiction if it is supposed that the Harappans were Dravidians or non-Aryans, because Śiva in Hindu tradition is a *brāhmin*, very much an "Aryan" concept. (Curiously enough, the place where the Harappan civilization was discovered in the past century by the British was called Brahminabad or Brahmin City. Could this be more than mere symbolism?) A final remark in this context is that the Harappans used a year of six seasons, as in the Ṛg Veda, and further used a sixty-year (Jovian) cycle, which has been an ancient Hindu tradition.

3. The goddess associated with a tiger in a Kalibangan cylinder seal compares closely with a cylinder seal from Shahdad (Iran), also depicting a goddess. This compares with seals showing a goddess on a tiger (or lion) from Bactria.[34] All this is easily understandable in terms of Durgā of Hindu mythology. This also shows links with Sumeria, because until comparatively recently, cylinder seals were exclusively associated with that region.
4. The eagle-headed deity from Baluchistan of the second millennium B.C. compares with the motifs of similar deities fighting serpents found in Greater Iran, with the variation of a human head and a bird body (both considered to be the same), again fighting serpents.[35] This could be the echo of bird-men type sculptures from the much earlier epoch at Nevali Cori. All this is again readily understandable in terms of the bird Garuḍa, the vehicle of Víshṇu (the Sun) of Hindu mythology, and an enemy of serpents.
5. The Harappan seal found at Altyn Depe shows a link between central Asia and the Harappan civilization.[36] In fact, Prof. V. Masson on this basis suggested that the south central Asian people were, like the Harappans, Dravidian.
6. The pottery and terracotta figurines from southern Turkmenistan closely resemble similar objects from the Harappan civilization.[37]
7. The Vedic deities and Indo-Aryan names of Anatolia of the second millennium B.C. evidently show a close linkage.
8. The inhabitants of Greater Iran were Aryans while the language and culture of the Harappan civilization is also of the same origin. Furthermore, the racial types in southern India are no different from the Caucasian and Mediterranean types.

9. The burial material in southern Tajikistan of the second millennium is close to those in Indo-Aryan burials.[38]
10. All this can be tied up with the distinct Vedic influence at Nevali Cori in the form of a limestone sculpture of a head of a Vedic priest, going back to the eighth millennium B.C.

The picture that emerges from the above mosaic of evidence and dates is that in the eighth millennium B.C. or earlier a Vedic culture with Ṛg Vedic Sanskrit as its language was already apparent in Anatolia, and that it gradually diffused toward both east and west. For a few thousand years—maybe about five thousand years—the language, religion, and culture gradually evolved and changed. This picture is in harmony with very recent findings based on blood groups and languages—in fact, from Europe through the Mediterranean regions to India we have the ethnic caucasoid group.[39]

A model having some resemblances to the above was proposed rather recently by Renfrew.[40] But Renfrew's model conflicts with that of French scholar Dumézil[41] who had argued that the several similarities in the myths of diverse and very widespread Indo-European cultures could not be merely accidental or due to routine diffusion and contact, as is implied by Renfrew. Indeed this would be far-fetched. Dumézil, on the lines of Max Müller, went on to trace a common ancestry for the Indo-European people among the Kurgan Russians, circa 3000 B.C. Renfrew and Dumézil completed their work before some of the excavations and other evidence touched on in this discussion. The scheme proposed here, in a sense, reconciles these two views to some extent.

In the earlier models, however, the language of the Anatolian region in the eighth millennium was a hypothetical proto-Indo-European and not Ṛg Vedic Sanskrit. Apart from the doubts cast on glottochronology, it is possible that the rate of change of languages was slower the farther back in time we go. Such a very slow and relatively peaceful diffusion is in fact mirrored by the gradual development of the Mehrgarh civilization. It is also vindicated by the Harappan model of a vast civilization comprising a large number of coexisting chiefdoms.

This brings us to around the second millennium B.C. where again we see a vast number of connections. This is also the period of the latest Brāhmaṇas and the Upanishads and the earlier epic period of Hindu literature. Indeed the literature portrays a picture not so much of a centralized empire, but that of a number of loosely interlinked smaller kingdoms, in relative harmony, on the lines of the Harappan settlements. In fact, the names of a number of Hindu epic dynasty families, for example, the Kúrus, can be traced to Greater Iran. Similarly tribe or community names from Hindu epics like the Vṛikas can be traced right up to the Gurgan Plain.[42] The far-extending lion- or tiger-borne mother-goddess motifs, the eagle and serpent motifs, and the svastika motifs all support this view and can be understood against this background. Further, the "Old Indo-Aryan" language of the Harappans, in the context of the above scenario, suggests that the language, rather than being a precursor of Vedic Sanskrit, was a corruption of the latter due to passage of time and distance; the Indus Valley may not have been the epicenter of the then prevalent Vedic civilization, which was probably centered in adjacent Greater Iran.

There is in fact astronomical evidence for the above assertions. Two ancient Hindu astronomical texts, the Jyotisha Vedāṅga and the Pitāmaha Siddhānta (attributed to the hero scholar Bhīshma of the Mahābhārata), both dating to around the middle of the second millennium, are set in a latitude of about 35 degrees north, as can be deduced from the given relative length of the longest day of the year. This falls right inside Greater Iran. A few scholars have taken the unfounded and untenable view that this merely represents a trace of Babylonian astronomy. Others would be reluctant, again without much of a basis, to transplant the epic Hindu setting to Greater Iran. But the fact is that in the Mahābhārata itself, places such as Gandhāra, Kamboja (Afghanistan), and Sindh, and peoples such as the Yavanas, Valhikas, and so on, are featured. According to the longitude given by Varāhamihira, circa 500 B.C., Yavana (probably Ionia) would correspond to Alexandria while Valhika has been identified with Balkhash.[43]

Large-scale and possible violent migrations or invasions seem to be a feature more evident from the second millennium B.C. According to

Soviet archaeologists, it appears that only from the middle of the second millennium B.C. did active migrations of the steppe tribes of central Asia take place, and these tribes penetrated the erstwhile farming and settled cultures.[44] This situation is also mirrored in west Asia around the same time.

## CONCLUDING OBSERVATIONS

The very ancient date of around 10,000 B.C. proposed for the Ṛg Veda or Vedic culture now appears plausible in view of the epi-Paleolithic agricultural or proto-agricultural civilizations dating back to a similar or even earlier period. If, as European scholars have supposed, the Ṛg Vedic descriptions of invasions of the circular forts of the *dāsas* or aborigines are to be taken at all literally, couldn't these forts be identified with the circular dwellings of the Neolithic people in and around the Anatolian region?

In fact, the word Aryan of the Ṛg Veda is derived from the Sanskrit root meaning "to plow." What all this is about is lucidly expounded in several Purāṇas (for example, the Víshṇu Purāṇa) in their characteristic allegorical style. In a nutshell: From the thigh of King Vena, all the evil came out in the form of a black dwarf (that is, an aboriginal pygmy). From the king's right hand, came out a beautiful shining prince, Pṛithú, who, because of a famine, pursued Earth intending to slay it, as it would not yield its fruits. Earth finally relented. "Before his time there was no cultivation, no pasture, no agriculture, no highways for merchants, all these things originated [then]. . . . Where the ground was made level, the King induced his subjects to take up their abode. . . . Then proceeded all kinds of corn and vegetables upon which people now subsist. . . ."[45] Pṛthú's son was Manu of Hindu mythology, the progenitor of humankind. Thus the "Arya" of the Ṛg Veda would represent, rather than an ethnic type, the very first agricultural people whence civilization itself began, sometime prior to about 10,000 B.C.[46]

In this connection, it is interesting to note that the term Aryan with its modern connotation is of rather recent coinage. Once the similarities between Sanskrit, Greek, Latin, German, and the Celtic languages were discovered by Sir William Jones, the term "Indo-Germanic" was coined by Bopp, the nineteenth-century German comparative philologist. This was later rechristened "Aryan," by Max Müller, from the Ṛg Vedic—supposedly racial—"Arya."[47]

But the Ṛg Veda and Vedic literature show a level of astronomy and science far ahead of that seen from about 2000 B.C. onward. Historians have, by and large, adopted a linear model of progress that has not always been true. There have been periods of regression in human civilization and human knowledge. It appears that very advanced but camouflaged astronomy in the Ṛg Veda slowly decayed, as its meaning was lost. In fact, even the earliest of Brāhmaṇas like the Aitareya Brāhmaṇa (circa 6000 B.C.) already begins to speculate on the possible meanings of the Ṛg Veda.

A final thought on the bifurcation in west Asia between the Indo-European and Semitic groups. The French philosopher Amaury de Riencourt theorizes that the Judeo-Christian concept of a (single) extra-cosmic God was the result of the abstraction of the concept of an all-powerful king of a kingdom.[48] It is quite interesting to note that the Hindu epic tradition, on the other hand, gives the picture of several kings coexisting, as possibly mirrored in the Harappan civilization. This is more in tune with the Hindu concept of an all-pervasive God, rather than a centralized one. Can the divergence of the two worldviews be found in these two models? There are of course interesting links between early Semitic gods and Vedic traditions. For example, the Semitic God Yahiveh corresponds to the Sun, Yahva, of the Ṛg Veda or the Elamite God; In Shushinak exactly corresponds to the Sanskrit In Ṡesanāga, the Serpent Lord (this being supported by archaeological evidence). (*In* in old Sanskrit means "Lord.")[49]

But there is a curious linguistic feature that might just symbolize this bifurcation. The Judeo-Christian traditions are from Abraham (of the second millennium B.C.), a word that could be interpreted as being derived from *a-brahman*, with brahminism being identical to the Ṛg Vedic tradition.

# 10

# Víshṇu as Astronomical Symbol from the Vedas to the Purāṇas

Víshṇu appears in the hymns of the most ancient Hindu literature, the Ṛg Veda. There, however, he is not the prominent deity that he later became. In fact, in the Ṛg Veda he only appears in about five full hymns and partially in another hymn as against 250 hymns devoted to Índra.

Vishṇu's role in overcoming the *asuras*, jointly with Índra, is already there in the Ṛg Veda. In the Brāhmaṇas, which exemplify the almost equal battle between the *devas* (gods) and the *asuras*, Víshṇu appears in a dwarf form to overcome the *asuras* by trickery. All this climaxes in the Purāṇas in Víshṇu taking the form of the Vāman avatar (or manifestation as Vāman).

The Hindu gods and their deeds are personifications and allegorical descriptions of perfectly meaningful natural phenomena; these allegories camouflage a deep understanding of these phenomena. If the concept of *devas* and *asuras* is probed, the *devas*—literally, the "bright ones"—are the day, that is, the bright half of the day; the *asuras*—literally, "those who have not quaffed the draught of nectar or Sóma or bright light"—represent darkness. Further, as pointed out previously, the day could be that of mortals, the usual twenty-four-hour day; or it could be the day of the manes (forefathers), one month with, by analogy, the bright half and the dark half; or it could be the day of the gods, the year, with the bright and dark halves representing the annual motion of the Sun from the winter solstice to the summer solstice and back again to the winter solstice.[1] The battle between the *devas* and *asuras* is therefore the almost equal "battle" between the bright halves and the dark halves.

In the Ṛg Veda the identification of Víshṇu, literally, "the all-pervading," with the Sun, whose rays penetrate everywhere, is already obvious and universally accepted. This is the key to a first understanding of many of the Víshṇu myths in Vedic and post-Vedic literature. Thus, as we have seen, the Índra-Vṛitrá battle of the Ṛg Veda in which Víshṇu aids the former is really a deliberately camouflaged description of Earth's atmosphere, Índra, dispelling the darkness, Vṛitrá, with the help of sunlight. In the Purāṇas, sunlight, or Víshṇu, enters Indra's weapon (the Vájra) with which he vanquishes Vṛitrá.[2]

We have also seen that the Purāṇic legend of Samudra manthana, the churning of the ocean in which Víshṇu helps the gods to overcome the *asuras*, is really a description of the rotation of Earth, once the symbols are identified: the self-coiling churning rope, the serpent Vāsuki, denotes Earth's rotation; Víshṇu in the form of Kūrmá the tortoise, supporting Earth, represents the gravitational force-aspect of the Sun, which causes the slow annual motion of Earth and so on.[3] (Interestingly, there is another symbol here: the tortoise contracts or withdraws into its shell, like the contractive-attractive gravitational force.) Víshṇu himself rests on the serpent Anantá (literally "endless"), which denotes the Sun's rotation.

Similarly the Trivikrama aspect of Víshṇu, denoting his three wide strides, would represent the three illumined regions of Earth, namely, the morning twilight zone, the daylight zone, and the evening twilight zone, while Bali, the *asura* of darkness, is relegated to the night or lower zone of Earth. One could also argue that the three steps of Víshṇu could represent the sunlit zone of Earth, the illumined Moon, which shines by sunlight, and the Sun itself in heaven; or even the Sun at the winter solstice, when days are shortest, the Sun at the equinoxes when the length of the day equals the length of the night, and the Sun at summer solstice, when the day is longest. Another explanation that has been put forward, namely, that the three steps denote the common points of the lunar (that is, *nákshatra*) and solar zodiacs is not so convincing.

Continuing in this vein, it can be seen how most of the Víshṇu symbolisms and myths from the Vedas and other Purāṇas can be consistently interpreted in terms of a deep understanding of the Sun, the phases of the Moon, and the solar system and its general features once the allegory is understood. As discussed in chapter 3, the heliocentric model of the solar system and other related concepts were already known in Ṛg Vedic times.

It has been noted above that the tortoise (Kūrmá) avatar of Víshṇu pertains to the Sun's gravitational support of Earth. This is also the significance of the fish (Mátsya) avatar of Víshṇu. Here the Sun in the form of a fish tethers Earth in the form of a boat or a ship and pulls it through the waters of space. This is additional proof of the fact that the ancient seers knew of Earth's annual motion. Incidentally, the terms "spaceship earth" and "ocean of space" are back in vogue in modern times. The Víshṇu Purāṇa clearly refers to Víshṇu influencing the motions of the planets.[4]

There is a popular belief that the avatars of Víshṇu are the different stages of evolution of life. This appears rather forced, compared to the simple and self-consistent explanations given above.

The attributes of Víshṇu can also be understood astronomically. For example, his Sudarśaná disc *(cakrá)* represents the wheel of time in an astronomical rather than a philosophical sense. It is described as having six naves representing the six seasons or two-month pairs (of Vedic times); twelve spokes, namely, the twelve months of the year; and two yokes, namely, the revolutions of the Moon and Earth, which give rise to the month and year, respectively.[5]

The five-jeweled Vaijayanta necklace worn by Víshṇu represents the five jewel-like planets that can be seen with the naked eyes and that orbit Víshṇu as if tied in a garland. Similarly, the lotus that sprouts from his navel (whence Padmanābha, or "lotus from navel") whose petals close in the evening can also be explained meaningfully: the Víshṇu Purāṇa describes Earth as a lotus. The reason is clear—with sunrise there is light, as if the lotus has opened up, and at sunset there is darkness, as if the lotus has closed. The eight petals of the lotus represent the eight directions, that is, the four cardinal directions and the four intermediate directions. The Āditya Hṛídayaṁ in the Rāmāyaṇa describes the Sun as one who causes the lotus to open out.[6]

That the Moon shines by reflected sunlight, and that the phases of the Moon are caused by the orbital motion of the Moon, were well known. These facts are described in several Vedic and Purāṇic passages, whether it be, for example, the Ṡatápatha Brāhmaṇa, the Mārkaṇḍeya Purāṇa, or the Víshṇu Purāṇa, and so on. This is exactly the meaning of the story of the sage Átri and his son Sóma, or the Moon. It has been pointed out earlier in another context that Átri is a personification of the Sun.[7] In fact, Átri dispels darkness and can be identified with Agní.[8] His son, the Moon, was married to the twenty-seven daughters of Dáksha, that is, the twenty-seven *nákshatras* or lunar asterisms along the Moon's path.[9] As the Moon begins to wane and gets diminished by disease he returns to his father Átri, who frees him from his illness and releases him again; that is, a new monthly cycle begins when the Moon is in conjunction with the Sun on the day of the new Moon. More explicitly, the Mārkaṇḍeya Purāṇa (canto 78) states explicitly that the Sun is the maker of the day, twilight, and moonlight.[10] The Víshṇu Purāṇa states clearly that the Moon is cherished by the Sushumnà ray of the Sun.[11] Similarly, the story of the churning of the ocean in which Víshṇu cuts the *asura* Rāhú (who tries to gobble up the Sun) into two parts is perfectly clear if these two parts are seen as representing the nodes where eclipses take place. In fact, this story has an exact parallel with the interpretation of the story of Kārttikeya in the Mahābhārata in which Kārttikeya splits into two parts, forming the diametrically opposite lunar asterisms Kṛíttikā and Viśākha, exactly as the two nodes Rāhú and Ketu are diametrically opposite. (Eclipses take place at the nodes.)[12]

Another peculiar attribute of Víshṇu is the *śrīvatsa* mark, described as a whorl of hair. This is a very apt description of a sunspot. Sunspots, incidentally, can even be seen with the naked eye around sunrise or sunset time. Sunspots, in fact, have been known since the earliest times; in the Ṛg Veda itself the Sun is referred to as a spotted or mottled bull or bullock.[13]

Further insight into the role of the Sun in nature is given in the descriptions of the water cycle, beginning in the Ṛg Veda (1.164) and continuing in the Purāṇas, as seen in the Āditya Hṛídayaṁ of the Rāmāyaṇa and the Víshṇu Purāṇa. Names for the Sun like Ravi and Kapi literally mean "one who drinks the waters." For example, the Víshṇu Purāṇa (chapter 11) says, "the moisture of Earth which the Sun attracts by his rays, he again parts with for the fertilization of the grain and the nutriment of all terrestrial creatures."[14] Thus the role of the Sun, both in astronomical and physical phenomena, was well known.

Equally surprising is the fact that from the time of the Ṛg Veda it was recognized that the Sun was a star, like the other stars in the sky. The Ṛg Veda in fact, describes the Sun as the daytime star. Interestingly, the Sun is described as being yellow-green (hari) and also as being a dwarf (Vāman). In modern astrophysics the Sun is known as a yellow dwarf or subdwarf star.

In the light of the above comments, one can now recognize the scientific facts in the various names of Víshṇu that Bhīshma summarized in the Víshṇu Sahásranāma (or thousand epithets of Víshṇu) of the Śānti Parva of Mahābhārata.[15] For instance:

1. Sthāṇu, one who is steady and immovable, indeed, as is the Sun at the center of the solar system. The same sense is contained in other names of the Sahásranāma like Sthira, Ácyuta, Acala, Dhruvá, and so on.
2. Bhūtâdi, the source of all elements. Surprisingly, in the modern astrophysical sense this is correct.
3. Samvatsara, the year. In fact, the Sun is the maker of the year.
4. Aha-Saṃvartaka, who regulates the succession of day and night.

5. Āvartana, one who sends the worlds whirling round. This is a correct description of the planets going around the Sun, owing to the Sun's gravitational pull.
6. Dharaṇī Dharāḥ, one who supports the world, that is, Earth. Again this is a correct description, and the same sense is contained in other names of the Sahasranāma like Mahidharah, Medinipati, Dharaṇidhara, Bhāravṛitta, and so on.
7. Śipiviṣṭah, rays of sunlight, which are called Śipi because they consume the waters of the oceans and seas, and the Sun who dwells in these watery rays is so called.
8. Candrāmśuḥ, the rays of the Moon; it is sunlight that is reflected off the Moon as moonlight.
9. Yugādikṛit, one who causes the periods of time. There are many other names with the same connotation in the Sahasranāma like Yugá Vaṛtana, Ṛitú, Kāla, Sudarśana (refer to the Sudarśana discus of Víshṇu discussed above), all referring to the fact that the year, the seasons, and so on, are caused by the Sun.
10. Nákshatri, refers to the fact that the Sun is a star. There are other such names in the Sahasranāma denoting the same, for example, Tāraḥ (star).
11. Saṅkarṣano'cyuta, is a significant name that denotes one who while remaining fixed attracts other objects to himself.
12. Vanamāli, because Víshṇu wears the five-jeweled garland called Vaijayanti, which represents the five planets visible to the naked eye.
13. Śrīvatsavaksha, one who wears the Śrīvatsa mark on his chest, namely, the sunspots.
14. Tejovṛṣa, one whose energy is the cause of rainfall. This is also the meaning of names like Ravi, Kapi, and so on.
15. Saptajihvāḥ, one who has seven tongues of flame (elaborated upon for example, in the Māṇḍūkya Upanishad). A simple explanation for this epithet, as with other names such as Saptaidhāh, would be the seven colors of the Sun's rays.

16. Adhṛtah, one who, being the support of worlds like Earth, is not supported himself by anything external. Again astronomically this is correct. The same sense is contained in names like Adhātā, Lokādhiṣthānam, and so on.

It is not out of place here to refer to another curious Purāṇic legend, one that can be very meaningfully interpreted in the context of the above remarks. This is the story of Índra and the brahmin boy. In a nutshell, the story is that when Índra had grown arrogant, Víshṇu in the form of a brahmin boy *à la* Vāman, appeared before him and asked, "Ṡākra (Índra) how manifold is creation? How manifold indeed is the one? . . . How many are the eggs of Brahmā; how many are the Brahmās, Vishṇus, and Śivas within the eggs? How many the Índras? . . . If motes of dust and drops of rain can be numbered, Oh, Overlord of the Gods, still there shall be no number to the Índras, as the wise know well."[16]

The curious speech can be understood in terms of the grand cosmic view in Vedic and Purāṇic literature that is consistent with modern ideas of several universes, each existing for thousands of millions of years.[17] More specifically, it takes on an even more modern astrophysical connotation if it is remembered that Índra is also identified with the star Jyéshṭha (literally "first" or "biggest") or Antares.[18] Now, Antares is indeed the largest conceivable type of star, what astronomers call a supergiant. It is millions of times the size of the Sun or Víshṇu, which although important, as pointed out earlier, is a small subdwarf star. But however big Antares might be, there are billions of such supergiants in the universe!

To conclude, it appears that all the otherwise peculiar myths, symbols, and names of Víshṇu are capable of a perfectly straightforward and cogent interpretation in terms of modern astronomical and astrophysical views of the Sun and the solar system.

# 11

# A Date and Place for the Mahābhārata

The date of the Mahābhārata period has been a matter of debate for several decades. An early date of around 3000 B.C. to a date of around the beginning of the Christian era have been proposed by several scholars.[1] A number of scholars have also proposed a date of around 1400 B.C.[2] Much of this work has been on the basis of literary and calendric interpretations.

On the basis of several interrelated astronomical references in the Jyotisha Vedāṅga, Paitāmaha Siddhānta, and the Mahābhārata itself, as well as on the basis of the astronomical observations of Parāśara, the father of Vyāsa, composer of Mahābhārata, I would like to propose a date of around 1350 B.C. for the events in the Mahābhārata. The unraveling of an astronomical symbolism also confirms this period and gives the date of June 24, 1311 B.C., for the total solar eclipse that was witnessed during the war.

These astronomical references are also shown to give, independently, a latitude of about 35 degrees north for the locale of the Mahābhārata. This latitude encompasses the region from Turkey and western Iran to southern Turkmenistan through Afghanistan and Kashmir down to the Indus Valley.

The period and place are compatible with literary sources and archaeological data, and would help to explain the reasons for the lack of archaeological evidence at traditionally accepted sites like Kúrukshetrá. This is an interesting problem for archaeologists.

## THE ASTRONOMICAL EVIDENCE

The Paitāmaha Siddhānta, containing the astronomical principles attributed to Bhīshma, a well-known exponent of the calendar in the Mahābhārata, gives the winter solstice in the *nákshatra* or lunar asterism Dhánishṭha (Delphinus), and also gives a latitude of 35 degrees, which can be calculated on the basis of the ratio of the longest day to the shortest day in the year.[3] Winter solstice at Dhánishṭha took place around 1350 B.C.

The Jyotisha Vedāṅga, one of the oldest suriving Indian astronomical texts, also gives the same date and latitude.[4]

Interestingly, the Mahābhārata also independently mentions that time begins with the *nákshatra* Dhánishṭha, while Bhīshma refers to the five-year cycle (*yugá*) mentioned in the Jyotisha Vedāṅga and the Paitāmaha Siddhānta.[5]

Two independant astronomical references by Parāśara, father of Vyāsa, the composer of, and a participant in, the Mahābhārata can be dated to around 1350 B.C. One is again the reference to the winter solstice in the lunar asterism Dhánishṭha.[6] The other is his statement that the star Agástya, or Canopus, when it enters the lunar asterism Hásta (Corvus), rises with the Sun; and it sets with the Sun when it is in the lunar asterism Róhiṇī.[7] This took place in 1350 B.C. at around 35 degrees north latitude. Indeed the five-year cycle referred to above can also be traced to Parāśara. What is even more remarkable is that in the Víshṇu Purāṇa, Parāśara explicitly expounds the lengths of the longest day and shortest day of the year, both of which correspond only to the latitude of 35 degrees. (These lengths are mentioned in terms of the ancient Indian time unit, the *muhūrtá*.) There is thus perfect agreement with regard to period and latitude from diverse astronomical references.

There is a further astronomical symbolism that enables us to pinpoint the time and place even more accurately. To appreciate this, one has to remember the legend of Vyāsa dictating the epic to Gaṇēśa, who was supposed to write it down, but only after comprehending the dictation. To gain time Vyāsa deliberately constructed his *kūṭas* or puns. One such pun is immediately evident in the identification of Bhīshma with the Sun.[8] First, the story of the birth of the eight Vásus to Gáṅgā, only the last of whom, Bhīshma, would live for long on Earth, exactly parallels the Ṛg Vedic Áditi and her eight offspring, only the last of whom, Mārtāṇḍa (Sun) would live (RV 10.72.8). Bhīshma commanded the Kaurava army for ten days. These are the ten days when the Sun is near the summer solstice and when its declination remains practically constant before it decreases as it begins its southern descent. As Indian scholar Mukherjee points out, Hindu Jyotisha (astrological) works attribute to Mārtāṇḍa extreme power for ten days.[9] Bhīshma, sunlike, is backed by the ten thousand solar troops, the Nārāyaṇi Sena, symbolizing the thousands of rays of the Sun. At the end of the tenth day, sunlike Bhīshma falls, but like the Sun, he waits for *uttarâyaṇa*—which begins when the Sun reaches winter solstice—to die, again like the Vedic Sun, and so on.

Further, in the Great War, Bhīshma is attacked by the hero Árjuna from behind Ṡikhaṇḍi. Interestingly, the Great Bear or Sapta Ṛíshis is also known as Citrá Ṡikhaṇḍi. Its first two stars are in line with Magha (Regulus), which marked the summer solstice, and at which point the Sun, or Bhīshma identified with the Sun (as explained below), falls; the lunar asterisms behind the summer solstice Magha are the Árjunīs, or Phalgunīs, both of which have a well-known identification with Árjuna (being his birth asterism). According to the Purāṇas, the Sapta Ṛíshis (or Ṡikhaṇḍi) was in the lunar asterism Magha at about the time of the reign of Parikshit, Árjuna's grandson.

This complicated Vyāsa *kūṭa* or pun (as explained later) would mean that the summer solstice was in Regulus, which again took place around 1350 B.C.! Moreover, this would mean automatically that the winter solstice was, as pointed out earlier, in Dhánishṭha, when the Sun, or Bhīshma identified with the Sun, would die. Interestingly enough, not only is the deity Vásu associated with the *nákshatra* Dhánishṭha, with Bhīshma himself being a Vásu, but also Áditi, the mother of the Vásus, is referred to as Dhánishṭha Mātā (mother of Delphinus).

This astronomical symbolism goes beyond a mere reiteration of the period of the Mahābhārata. It also gives us the date of the Mahābhārata war—it took place around June 21, when the Sun was at the summer solstice. Another astronomical event then enables us to pinpoint the year. This event is the total solar eclipse in the afternoon that caused the darkness that led Jayadratha to think that the Sun had set, and which ultimately led to his being slain by Árjuna. Interestingly, in the period 1800 B.C. to 800 B.C., only one total solar eclipse was seen in the afternoon around June 21 from anywhere in or around India.[10] This is the eclipse of June 24, 1311 B.C. This total solar eclipse was seen in the late afternoon from areas near about Kabul and Peshawar, which again have a latitude of about 35 degrees![11]

Incidentally, the statement that the Sapta Ṛíshis were in Magha[12] is perfectly intelligible in light of the above. But the later tradition that has this phenomenon keep changing is dubious and astronomically incorrect.

## LITERARY SOURCES AND TRADITION

Several literary references support the above conclusions. For example, the Víshṇu Purāṇa clearly mentions that 1,015 years elapsed between the birth of Parikshit, the grandson of Árjuna, and the coronation of Nanda who lived around 300 B.C. A few Purāṇas, however, give the figure as 1,050 years.

References in the Mahābhārata, Víshṇu Purāṇa, and other texts make mention of places around a latitude of 35 degrees and of the peoples living there, for example, Gandhāra and Kamboja (in Afghanistan), Kashmir, and even China. The peoples referred to include the Gandhāras, the Śakas (from Śakadvīpa near Afghanistan), Yavanas (or westerners), Tushāras (Tohara, Tukhara; the Tocharians of Chinese Turkistan; Tocharian, an Indo-European language, is now extinct), the Pahlavas of Iran, and several others. In fact, the Mahābhārata confers Vedic status to the Aryan domains of the Gandhāras, the Pahlavas, the Tushāras, and even the Yavanas. Interestingly, the Achaeans (Egyptian, Akaivasa, Hittite, and Ahhijava), of ancient Greece used iron, cremated their dead, and had Olympian gods: Uranus and Zeus, for example, are derived from Váruṇa and Dyaus. Also, as Wilford, a British indologist of the nineteenth century, pointed out, the sacred words uttered in the Eleusinian mystery rites were pure Sanskrit, namely, Canx, Om, Pax or Kāṅkshá, Om, Pakshá.[13]

It is also explicitly mentioned that Parāśara was from Śakadvīpa, as it is also known that the great Sanskrit grammarian Pāṇini himself is from Gandhāra. According to tradition the Pāṇḍavas are associated with shrines in Peshawar (formerly Puruṣapura and later Puruṣawar), for example, the Pañcatīrtha and in Kashmir, for example, the Mārtāṇḍa and Mamalleswar temples.[14] The antiquity of some of these temples is traced back traditionally to about 1350 B.C. This tradition is corroborated by, or partly originates from, the work of the twelfth-century Kashmiri historian Kalhana, who probably based his conclusions on the strength of the Nílamat Purāṇa. According to tradition again, Janmejaya, the son of Parikshit, performed the famous snake sacrifice at Takshaśila (Taxila) in the same general area.[15]

## ARCHAEOLOGICAL SOURCES

The above scenario gets support from several archaeological sources. It is well known that, around 1500 B.C., a vast area from Anatolia in Turkey through Iran and central Asia and down to Afghanistan and the Indus Valley had strong Sanskritic influences. In fact, it was suggested in chapter 9 that, based on these considerations, the events depicted in Indian epics took place in this region.

The archaeological evidence from Anatolia in Turkey consists of the well-known Boghuz Koi inscriptions of around 1400 B.C. that mention Vedic deities, the so-called Indo-Aryan Hittite, Mittani, Kassite, and other tribes that worshiped Hindu deities, the manuscript of the treatise on horses by Kikkuli that employed several Sanskrit terms like *ékavaṛtana*, *dvevartana*, and so on.

It has also been recognized that, from about 2000 B.C., sites like Tepe Hissar III in Iran, Namazga V in southern Turkmenistan, and also regions like Dashly III in Afghanistan—in fact, a vast region extending from the Gurgan Plains near the Caspian Sea through southern Turkmenistan (Namazga, Altyn Depe), Murghab Delta (ancient Margiana, Togolok, etc) and ancient Bactria including northern Afghanistan (Dashly) right up to the Indus Valley—show uniform cultural traits constituting the Bronze Age Namazgah V culture.[16] Large quantities of weapons and remains of chariots found there have led scholars to conclude that an Aryan military elite dominated this area. At Dashly III a fire temple (circa 2000 B.C.) with three concentric circular walls (*à la* Trípura) has come to light, and there is evidence of another such temple as well. At Togolok 21 yet another fire temple has been found (circa 1800 B.C.) where the ancient Vedic Sóma ritual was also practiced. In addition, a goddess associated with a tiger in a Kalibangan cylinder seal compares closely with a cylinder seal from Shahdad (Iran), also depicting a goddess. This compares with seals from Bactria showing a goddess on a tiger (or lion). The images on these seals are easily cognate with Durgā of Hindu mythology.

The Harappan seal found at Altyn Depe shows that there was contact between central Asia and the Harappan civilization. On this basis Professor Masson has suggested that the south central Asian people were, like the Harappans, Dravidian.

Pottery and terracota figurines from southern Turkmenistan closely resemble similar objects from the Harappan civilization. The burial materials found in southern Tajikistan from the second millennium are close to those in Indo-Aryan burials.

Moreover, the names of a number of Hindu dynastic families, for example, the Kúrus, can be traced to the Iranian region. Similarly, names of tribes or communities from the epics like the Vṛíka can be traced right up the Gurgan Plains. The widespread lion- or tiger-borne mother-goddess motifs, other eagle and serpent motifs, and the svastika motifs of the Indus Valley all support the above scenario that the Mahābhārata events took place in a region around Iran, Afghanistan, and the Indus Valley area in the second millennium B.C.

Professor Rao's marine archaeological excavations confirm the existence of Kṛishṇá's undersea city of Dvārakā dating back to around 1500 B.C.[17] Indeed, the Mahābhārata describes graphically the submergence of Dvārakā. Rao's work also reveals that the language of the Indus seals was Sanskritic and ties in well with the fire altars and other archaeological evidence in the Indus Valley. Moreover, the marine excavations also reveal links with some of the above far-flung places. Rao's work pushes back the date of iron implements to about 1700 B.C., which would be the outer limit for the Mahābhārata period, since such implements or weapons were used.

Equally significant is the Hisse-Borala inscription, on the basis of which it can be concluded that the Mahābhārata war took place between 1280 B.C. and 1414 B.C.

A very ancient manuscript discovered in the adjoining region of Yarkand, in China, and which expounds ancient Indian astronomy, is also very suggestive. This work is attributed to an ancient Indian scholar Pushkarasāri. It is not at all surprising that the Chinese *hsieu* are so close to the Indian *nákshatras.*

Another interesting piece of evidence that supports the above scenario is connected with the legend already referred to of the elephant-headed Gaṇêśa writing down the Mahābhārata to the dictation of Vyāsa. Indeed, a metal plate depicting the elephant-headed deity holding a quill has been found in Luristan (western Iran) and has been dated to around 1200 B.C. to 1000 B.C., while some other Luristan bronzes have motifs from the closely related Avesta.[18]

On the one hand, no convincing archaeological evidence for the Mahābhārata has been found in and near traditional places like

Kúrukshetrá. This has led some scholars to dismiss the Mahābhārata as a myth or to see it as a very small feud, vastly exaggerated in the epics. On the other hand, there is sufficient astronomical and other evidence to suggest that the battle and many of the events of the Mahābhārata took place in regions around Afghanistan, around 1350 B.C.

The evidence of the Aryan military elite of Namazgah is in fact closer to the descriptions in the Purāṇas and epics than those at places like Kúrukshetrá. The unsubstantiated theory of an Indo-Aryan invasion around 1500 B.C. has prevented a proper interpretation of all the findings and has clouded the facts. For instance, *this very period* (of around 1400 B.C.) and region (northwest frontier) have been attributed by some scholars to the composers of Ṛg Veda.[19] Further archaeological excavations, particularly in the areas indicated above, are called for and could provide key answers.

# 12

# Astronomy, Symbolism, and Ancient Indian Chronology: A Date for the Rāmāyaṇa

I have pointed out previously that the antiquity of Vedic literature and civilization has been grossly underestimated.[1] In fact, ancient Indian literature shows a continuing tradition of astronomy from 10,000 B.C. or earlier to the period of the Jyotisha Vedāṅga, about 1350 B.C.[2] It has also been pointed out that most of the so-called myths of ancient Indian literature are allegorical descriptions of very precise and well-comprehended astronomical phenomena.[3] What has been overlooked is the fact that some of these myths actually yield a clue to the dates of the events described in them. Let us examine some of these.

## The Prajāpati and Triśaṅku Myths

One of the earliest legends is that of Prajāpati cohabiting with his daughter Róhiṇī, who had assumed the form of a deer. This legend is elaborated upon in the Aitareya Brāhmaṇa of the Ṛg Veda; in fact, it has its origin in the Ṛg Veda itself.[4] Briefly put, Prajāpati was shot by an arrow with three parts as he became an animal *(mṛigá)* (or his head was replaced by an animal's head) for committing this sinful act, and his daughter, a deer, became the lunar asterism Róhiṇī or Aldebaran. This part of the astronomical symbolism is very transparent. Prajāpati is the constellation Orion the Hunter with three stars forming his waist; his head is the lunar asterism Mṛigáśira (literally, "head of the animal" or "animal head").

This legend conceals a lot more, however. Prajāpati has been explicitly identified in the Brāhmaṇas and elsewhere with a time period like the year. His planting his seed in his daughter Róhiṇī is really his planting the seed of a new year, that is, it denotes the beginning of the year with Róhiṇī at the winter solstice, something that took place around 10,000 B.C.[5] This is again corroborated by the legend of Índra pushing down the wheel of the Sun, which refers to the Sun's declination being stationary at the solstice around 10,000 B.C. As pointed out in chapter 7, this is what the story of Kārttikeya, Víśākha, Agní, and the wives of the seven sages (Sapta Ṛíshi) is all about, which again corroborates the above information.

We next come to the legend of King Triśaṅku (literally meaning "with three pegs or knots") of Ayodhyā, an ancestor of Rāma, that is recounted in the Rāmāyaṇa. The king Triśaṅku ascended heaven as a *caṇḍála*, or hunter, with the winter solstice being the gateway to heaven. (Even today, Vaikuṇṭha Ekādaśí, the day when the gates of heaven are open, is celebrated around winter solstice.) As mentioned above, around 10,000 B.C. Róhiṇī, who is also called Índra, was at the winter solstice; and Índra did not allow Triśaṅku in. Thereupon the sage Viśvāmitra began creating a duplicate universe, with another Índra, in order to send Triśaṅku there. This has reference to the star Jyéshṭha, also called Índra, which at that time was diametrically opposite at the summer solstice: in fact, both Róhiṇī and Jyéshṭha are very similar red stars. Thereupon Triśaṅku was allowed to hang midway. Triśaṅku (with the three pegs) is once again Orion the Hunter (with the three stars on the waist), and all this refers to the epoch 10,000 B.C. alluded to above! Significantly in that epoch all this happened in the southern sky, as mentioned in the legend, and this is a further justification for taking Róhiṇī at winter solstice.

In addition to these myths there are several other explicit astronomical references in the Vedas that independently confirm this antiquity of circa 10,000 B.C. for the Ṛg Veda. The question that then arises is this: Is it possible that there were settled communities around 10,000 B.C.?

Recent archaeological studies indeed suggest that this period, which is now called the Epipaleolithic period, did indeed have semi-agricultural communities, at the very least.[6]

## A DATE FOR THE RĀMĀYAṆA

This brings us to the Rāmāyaṇa, whose date of composition has been a matter of continuing debate and controversy.[7] The very fact that the Vedic sages and characters like Vásiṣṭha, Vīśvāmitra, Agástya, and others figure in the Rāmāyaṇa points to its belonging to the Vedic period, quite unlike the post-Vedic Mahābhārata.

One of the Vedic events is the battle between the gods (*devas*) and the demons (*asuras*). As discussed previously, this battle, which takes place at the termination of the *yugá* or epoch, is mentioned in the Ṛg Veda itself. The battle ended with a total solar eclipse that took place in the lunar asterism Tishyà or Púshya (Delta Cancri) around 7300 B.C.[8] The presiding deity of this asterism is Bṛíhaspáti, the preceptor of the gods. In some of the Brāhmaṇas, the *yugá* itself has been called Tishyà or Púshya Yugá.

All this fits in very well with the following facts of Rāma's history. He lived as the Tretā Yugá ended and the Dvāpara Yugá began. The battle between the gods and demons took place in his time. Further, in his time there was a total solar eclipse, again in the same Púshya asterism and with the conjunction of planets associated with the termination of the *yugá*.

It is quite evident and indeed not surprising that all these events point to the beginning of the *yugá* with the total solar eclipse in Púshya or Tishyà circa 7300 B.C., referred to in the Ṛg Veda. Of course, there are several other references in the Ṛg Veda that also yield this date. Several references point to the Aśvíns, or the lunar asterism Aśvíni in the constellation Aries, being at the winter solstice at the same time.[9]

Interestingly, there is archaeological evidence for this period. It comes in the form of the excavations at Nevali Cori in Anatolia, which depict a civilization of exactly the same period.[10] Among the sculptures and artifacts found there are the head with a striking resemblance to a Vedic priest, small sculptures of what could be monkeylike men and bird-men, and a pelican-like bird. At this site coexisting with advanced Megalithic people, what archaeologists have called an Anatolian elite priestly class, were primitive Neolithic (New Stone Age) people as well. Evidently at this place (and possibly elsewhere) and in this epoch there were two peoples separated by a wide chasm. This raises the interesting possibility that the Vānaras (or monkeys or half-men) of the Rāmāyaṇa could have been the primitive Neolithic people. Indeed, in the Rāmāyaṇa the Vānaras do fight with stones and boulders!

An interesting—and almost impossible to interpret—piece of art at Nevali Cori depicts twins dancing with a tortoise, a motif that has stumped archaeologists. This ideogram has a simple astronomical interpretation, in terms of the above considerations, when we remember that according to Vedic literature Prajāpati, the marker of time, moved slowly, as does the tortoise. With the dance interpreted as the precessional motion and Prajāpati as a tortoise being identified with the beginning of the year at the winter solstice, it is easy to see that the motif above refers to the twin Aśvíns appearing at the winter solstice around 7300 B.C., the exact date of the excavations.

So the Rāmāyaṇa is based on astronomical and possibly historical events circa 7300 B.C. extracted from the Vedas. The Vedas themselves were not meant to be epics, though there are allusions to names like Rāma, Sītā, Janaka, and others in the Ṛg Veda. Indeed, according to tradition, Vālmīki, the composer of Rāmāyaṇa, was the first poet and the Rāmāyaṇa was one of the earliest poems.

It is also interesting to note that the Greek Megasthenes quotes a tradition dating the origin of the Ikshvākú dynasty of Rāma to about 6500 B.C., and there is a Zoroastrian tradition that places the vernal equinox in Tistrya or Tishyà around 7300 B.C.

## THE BRĀHMAṆA EPOCH

There is a continuing tradition of astronomy in the epoch of the Brāhmaṇas, from the Aitareya Brāhmaṇa, for example, which gives a date of about 6000 B.C., (Áditi or the asterism Púnarvasu, that is, Castor and Pollux, at the vernal equinox), through the Śatápatha Brāhmaṇa, which gives a date of around 2500 B.C. with Kṛ́ttikā or the Pleiades at the vernal equinox.[11] Interestingly, one of the Indus seals belonging to this period shows the seven sages and Agní (fire) associated with the Kṛ́ttikā legend, a close parallel to the tortoise-and-twins ideogram of Nevali Cori. There is also a curious passage in the Mahābhārata that refers to the fact that though the Kṛttikā period was over, it came back again because people wanted it[12]—reference to a second Kṛ́ttikā period can now be easily understood. The first Kṛ́ttikā period (as explicitly mentioned) was around 8300 B.C. when Kṛ́ttikā was at the winter solstice; the second was when Kṛ́ttikā was at the vernal equinox.[13]

## THE MAHĀBHĀRATA PERIOD

This brings us to the Jyotisha Vedāṅga and the Mahābhārata, both of which can be dated to around 1350 B.C.[14] In fact, the legend of Áditi and the eight Vásus in the Ṛg Veda has a parallel with the legend of the birth of Kṛishṇá and Bhīshma. The Bhīshma symbolism also gives the same date of around 1350 B.C. It may be pointed out that, traditionally, while the Rāmāyaṇa is associated with the beginning of the Dvāpara Yugá, the Mahābhārata is associated with the beginning of the next *yugá*, that is, the Kali Yugá, which agrees with the above scenario. The archaeological findings in what Parpola calls Greater Iran agree with the Mahābhārata period.[15]

In summary, it appears that ancient Indian literature and civilization can be roughly divided into four periods:

1. The early Vedic period with Róhiṇī or Aldebaran at the winter

solstice, about 10,000 B.C. or earlier.

2. The middle Vedic period with Aśvíni, or Alpha and Beta Arietis, at the winter solstice, around 7000 B.C. This is the period of the Rāmāyaṇa and the Dvāpara Yugá.
3. The late Vedic period with Kṛíttikā or the Pleiades at the vernal equinox, around 2500 B.C. This is the period of the Śatápatha Brāhmaṇa and the Indus civilization.
4. The post-Vedic period of around 1400 B.C. This is the period of the Mahābhārata and Kali Yugá.

# 13

# The Indus Civilization—An Astronomical Perspective

There are many parallels between the Indus and the "Hindu"—that is, Vedic and Purāṇic—traditions that point to a continuity of civilization. The figurine of a mother goddess in a miniature temple-type enclosure found in houses even today is one such example, and the important continuing tradition of yoga is another.[1]

In addition, there are some seals that show an obvious link with Hindu tradition: the svastika seals of the Indus civilization are already anticipated around 4000 B.C., or earlier, at Mehrgarh; the pipal leaves on some of these seals can be linked to the holy pipal tree of Vedic times.

An interesting enigma in this connection is the statue, now in Pakistan, of the Indus priest or priest-king that has a band with a circular object on the forehead. There is hardly any clue what this could be. In the Mahābhārata, however, after the great war, Aśvatthāma, one of the prominent priest-warriors, is chased and caught by the Pāṇḍavas. As a mark of his surrender, Aśvatthāma gives away the *maṇí*, or jewel, on his forehead. This was clearly a symbol of his status. It is tempting to infer from this that an object on the forehead was indeed a status symbol of noble priests or scholars.

More specifically, the scale found at Mohenjadaro has markings in the decimal system, or, more correctly, in the scale of ten as in the Vedic tradition that starts with the Ṛg Veda itself. This also seems to be true of weights.[2]

## THE INDUS, VEDIC, AND PURĀṆIC ASTRONOMICAL TRADITIONS

There also seems to be continuity between the astronomical and calendrical concepts of the Indus and the Vedic and Purāṇic civilizations. Indeed, many of these concepts are still a living tradition in India.

For example, the Indus civilization had six seasons and the twelve-year Jovian (or Jupiter) cycle, and also the sixty-year cycle of five Jovian periods.[3] All this is found in the Vedic and Purāṇic tradition, particularly in connection with the Áṅgirasá, which compellingly leads to the identification with Jovian cycles.[4] The Ṛg Veda (1.64) in fact refers to the five twelve-year cycles (of Jupiter).

In fact, the continuing tradition of the Kumbhá Melā is connected with the entry of Jupiter into Kumbhá Rāśi, or Aquarius—a tradition that originates from the time when the winter solstice was in that constellation, roughly around 3000 B.C., very much in the Indus period.

Let us take a closer look at this aspect. Kumbhá Melā, according to legend, commemorates the battle between the *devas* and the *asuras* or the churning of the ocean *(samudra manthana)* for the nectar of immortality or amṛíta.[5] Such an encounter takes place at the end of a *yugá* and at the beginning of a new *yugá*, which again takes place in the winter solstice.

In this instance, as the nectar came out in a pot *(kumbhá)*—the pot of Aquarius the Water Bearer—it was whisked away by the gods and drops fell (or the pot was placed) at Haridwar, Ujjain, Prayag (Allahabad), and Nasik. The Kumbhá festival itself is still celebrated every twelve years when the planet Jupiter enters the constellation Kumbhá, or Aquarius. Indeed the winter solstice was in Kumbhá around 3000 B.C., and that is a remarkable date because, according to Hindu tradition, the Kali Yugá epoch commenced in 3102 B.C. Not only calendric traditions but also references in the Brāhmaṇas as well as a statement by Ā́ryabhaṭṭa, the celebrated astronomer who lived circa A.D. 500, support this date.[6] Incidentally, Ā́ryabhaṭṭa gives the count in terms of the sixty-year Jovian cycle.

Today the main Kumbhá Melā takes place at Prayag at the confluence of the Gáṅgā, Yamuna, and the so-called mythical Sárasvatī rivers. It is now well known that during the Indus period the Sárasvatī River was very prominent, but dried up, as has been verified by remote sensing data.[7]

In this connection, it may be mentioned that the Mahābhārata (Vánaparva) reveals that the Āṇgirasa or Jovian cycle took over from Agní or Kṛíttikā, that is, the Pleiades (Agní is this asterism's deity). This will be touched upon a little later.

We next come to some of the Indus seals and their connection with the astronomy of the Vedic and Purāṇic tradition. Indeed, some of these seals could well be ideograms. The most famous are the Paśúpáti seals that were identified early on by Sir John Marshall as depicting Śiva. Interestingly, this can be interpreted astronomically in an accurate way. In the Víshṇu Purāṇa (chap. 5) it is stated that the heavenly course was made with animals having twenty-eight obstacles, which is a description of the twenty-eight *nákshatras* or lunar asterisms. (Interestingly, the word *zodiac* comes from *zodos*, which is Greek for "animal.") Further, the Paśúpáti seal shows Śiva in the yogic posture with two horns. The horns are a well-known symbol for the crescent moon. In fact, the Sanskrit word *śṛiṅga* (horns) also means crescent moon, and even today we talk about the horns of the Moon. So the Paśúpáti seal depicts lunar astronomy.

It may be mentioned here that the *liṅga* (phallus) motifs in the Indus civilization have a close parallel not only with the present *liṅga* cult but also with the Prajāpati legend that originates in the Ṛg Veda and that is elaborated in the Aitareya Brāhmaṇa and other Brāhmaṇas. This has been discussed elsewhere, but in brief, the legend describes the beginning of the year, which in very early times took place when the winter solstice was near Róhiṇī, or Aldebaran.[8]

The famous seal showing the seven priests and the fire altar is intimately connected with the Agní and the Kṛíttikā legend expressed in the Ṛg Veda and elaborated upon in later Brāhmaṇic and Purāṇic works.[9] Briefly, this legend refers to an original period when the winter solstice was in the Pleiades, that is, Kṛíttikā, which was around 8350 B.C., as it is explicitly stated in Taittirīya Saṃhita. Curiously enough, the vernal equinox in the Pleiades is described in the Ṡatápatha Brāhmaṇa, and it took place around 2350 B.C., which exactly coincides with the date of the Indus civilization. It may also be mentioned that the Mahābhārata contains a curious passage in which it is stated that the Kṛíttikā period came to an end but people wanted the Kṛíttikā to come back again.[10] The Mahābhārata legend alluded to earlier also reveals that Agní or Kṛíttikā was persuaded by the Áṅgirasá of the Jovian cycle to take over its function again.[11] This is in all probability a reference to the fact that Kṛíttikā once again became impoṛtant as the vernal equinox. The seal also shows a twig with two pipal leaves, which has been interpreted as the diametrically opposite *nákshatra* Víśākha (literally, "two branches") by Parpola, which is further confirmation of the identification of the seal with the Kṛíttikā legend of Mahābhārata.[12]

An interesting but difficult to interpret seal is the one that depicts two goats and an auroch. The auroch, it is accepted, denoted the beginning of the year.[13] The two goats, on the other hand, denote the Vedic Pūshán (being his carriers), the deity of the lunar asterism Revatī, in Pisces. So, as I have pointed out elsewhere, this ideogram would represent the beginning of the year with the winter solstice at Revatī, which took place around 4400 B.C., the date of the Mehrgarh svastika seals. Interestingly, the beginning of the year at Revatī is also referred to in the Mārkaṇḍeya Purāṇa (canto 75). This interpretation suggests the possibility that the Harappan civilization might go back to around 4000 B.C., which is entirely plausible on archaeological grounds.

We next come to the mother goddess (cylinder) seal found at Kalibangan. This motif is also to be found in western Asia, for example, at Catal Huyuk, around 6000 B.C. This has an exact astronomical meaning if we notice first that the constellation Virgo the Lady is atop the constellation Leo the Lion, and that, moreover, the winter solstice was at Spica or Citra in Virgo exactly at the same time, around 6000 B.C. This tradition continues today in the form of Durgā known as Sin̲havāhanī, the lion- (or at times tiger-) borne mother goddess.

In a similar astronomical vein one could interpret the Śiva or Rudra and bull seals. Rudra is the deity of the *nákshatra* Arudra, or Betelgeuse, which is part of the Prajāpati constellation (Orion), which faces Taurus the Bull. Around 4000 B.C., in fact, the vernal equinox was at Arudra, whereas the winter solstice was there around 10,000 B.C. Even today in Indian temples Śiva's bull, Nandi, faces the *liṅga* (phallus), which is Śiva in the form of Prajāpati. (The reference here is to the legend, elaborated in the Aitareya Brāhmaṇa, of Prajāpati planting his seed in his daughter Róhiṇī, or Aldebaran.)

The beautiful seal depicting the mother goddess with the lotus has an immediate Purāṇic connotation; as is well known (cf. Mahābhārata, Śānti Parva), the lotus represents Mother Earth.[14]

We come finally to a very enigmatic Harappan seal that depicts an elephant-headed deity with legs of horses and bulls, the body of a tiger, and wearing horns in the manner of Śiva's attendants or *gaṇas* who are led by Gaṇêśa.[15] In this context it may be mentioned that Vyāsa, according to the medieval Arabic scholar, Alberuni, by tradition rediscovered writing and dictated the Mahābhārata to the elephant-headed Gaṇêśa, who then wrote it down. Much evidence points to this happening in the late Indus phase around 1300 B.C.[16] It is interesting that a Gaṇêśa-type deity with a writing quill has been depicted in a bronze work of Luristan in Iran going back to about the same date.[17] Interestingly, it is worth noting that the Brāhmi script, an ancestor of many Indian scripts, has a great deal of similarity with the Indus script, though phonetic identification is not unanimous.[18] It may also be noted that according to tradition it is again Brahma who invented the digits (numerals) that are of Indian origin.

## CONCLUDING REMARKS

Not only has the Indus civilization, without sufficient justification, been taken to be non-Vedic, but Vedic civilization itself has, again without sufficient justification, been dated as being post-Indus. The many common traits have been attributed to an absorption of the pre-Vedic Indus beliefs into the Vedic tradition. All this in recent years is being critically reexamined.

On the other hand, Indus astronomy is shown to be a part and parcel of the rather long and complex Vedic and Purāṇic tradition. So, the Indus civilization appears to be a phase in the evolution of the Vedic civilization from a pre-Indus period to present day Hinduism.

# GLOSSARY

***Agní (Fire)***
Epithet of the Sun.

**Amṛít**
Nectar of immoṛtality.

***Āraṇyaka***
Literature composed in forests (literally "aranya") speculating and elaborating upon the Vedic hymns.

***Aśvíns***
Twin deities who have been identified variously with day and night, Castor and Pollux, and so on. In this text they are identified with the planets Mercury and Venus.

***Atharva Veda***
The fourth of the ancient Vedic texts.

***Avatār***
The manifestation of God in an anthropomorphic form.

***Āyurveda***
Ancient Indian medical science.

***Brāhmaṇa***
A body of literature elaborating or giving commentary on the Vedic texts.

***Daitya, Rākshasa***
A demon, a force of evil or darkness.

***Deva***
God, forces of good (literally "bright ones").

***Dvāpara Yugá***
The third of the four epochs.

***Equinoxes***
The points where the equator and the ecliptic (the Sun's path) intersect. The Sun reaches these points at approximately March 21 and September 23 at which time the length of the day equals the length of the night.

***Gandharva***
A demigod, associated with music or rhythm in later literature.

***Índra***
The king of the gods or the bright ones, a prominent Vedic deity.

***Jyotisha Vedāṅga***
An ancient Hindu astronomical text dated circa 1350 B.C.

***Kali Yugá***
The last of the four epochs.

***Kálpa***
A very long period of time defined in Vedic literature. This equals 1,000 Mahāyugas, that is, 4,320,000,000 years.

***Kṛita Yugá***
The first of the four epochs.

***Liṅga***
Phallus or phallic symbol.

***Lunar year***
A year of 12 synodic months equalling 354 days.

***Mahābhārata***
A great Hindu epic, the longest poem in the world.

***Mahāyugá***
A long period of time equalling 4,320,000 years.

***Megalithic Period***
A period of civilization where large stone structures were used.

***Mitra***
A Vedic deity, precursor of the Roman Mithras.

***Nákshatra***
Lunar asterism, a group of stars (there being 27 such asterisms calibrating the Moon's path around Earth).

***Nā́satya***
A name for theAśvíns.

***Neolithic Period***
New Stone Age.

***Nivids***
Very ancient hymns or formulas found sketchily revealed in the Vedas and Vedic literature.

***Paleolithic Period***
An early part of the Stone Age.

***Pañcâṅga***
The indigenous Hindu calendar (literally "having five parts").

***Pitṛis***
Manes or souls of departed ancestors.

***Precession of Equinox***
A gradual shift of the equinoxes once in about 26,000 years, caused by the interplay of the gravitational forces of the Moon and the Sun on Earth.

***Purāṇas***
A body of literature, mythological in nature, composed long after Vedic literature.

***Rāmāyana***
A great Hindu epic.

***Rāśi***
A zodiacal sign.

***Ṛg Veda***
The oldest of the Vedas and the oldest extant Indo-European literature.

***Ṛíshi***
A sage or seer.

***Sāma Veda***
One of the ancient Vedic collections of hymns.

***Siddhântas***

Literary theories. A body of mathematical, astronomical literature dating back to the beginning of the Christian era (literally "theories").

***Sidereal month***

The time taken by the Moon to complete one orbit of Earth, about 27.3 days.

***Solstice***

The longest day or longest night of the year, around June 21 and December 21, respectively.

***Sóma***

A liquid, probably spirituous, referred to in the Vedas and not yet unambiguously identified. Also a name for the Moon.

***Sūrya***

A name for the Sun.

***Synodic month***

The period between two successive full moons or new moons, about 29.5 days.

***Taittirīya Saṃhita***

One of the four Vedas, also called Yajur Veda.

***Tretā Yugá***

The second of the four epochs.

***Tropical year***

The time it takes the Sun to return to an equinox (about 365.2422 days). This is the year of the seasons or the year of the calendar in present use.

***Upanishads***
A body of post Vedic literature, also called Vedānta (literally "end of the Vedas"), incorporating mostly philosophical and metaphysical discourses.

***Vájra***
The shining weapon of Índra, the lightning bolt.

***Váruṇa***
One of the early Vedic deities (literally "all encompassing," the precursor of the Hellinic Uranus).

***Víshṇu***
An early Vedic deity (literally "all-pervading") namely, the Sun.

***Vṛitrá***
A Vedic demon representing darkness, drought, etc.

***Yajur Veda***
One of the ancient Vedic collections of hymns.

***Yugá***
An epoch, a long period of time.

# NOTES

## INTRODUCTION

1. G. Santillana and H. Dechend on *Hamlet's Mill* (Boston: David R. Godine, 1977).
2. M. Haug, trans., *Aitareya Brāhmaṇam of the Ṛg Veda* (Varanasi: Bharatiya Publishing House, 1977).
3. J. Eggeling, *The Śatapatha Brāhmaṇa* (Delhi: Motilal Banarshidass, 1978).
4. R. T. H. Griffith, *The Hymns of the Ṛg Veda* (Varanasi: Chowkhamba Sanskrit Series, 1971).
5. C. Gay, *Ancient Ritual Stone Artifacts, Mexico-Guatemala-Costa Rica* (Gilly: Academie Royale De Belgique, 1995).
6. H. H. Wilson, trans., *Víshṇu Purāṇa* (Calcutta: Punthi Pustak, 1972), chap. 1.
7. F. E. Pargiter, trans., *Mārkaṇḍeya Purāṇa* (Varanasi: Indological Book House, 1981).
8. Wilson, *Víshṇu Purāṇa*, chap. 5.
9. P. C. Roy, trans., *Mahābhārata* (Calcutta: Oriental Publishing Company, 1956).

10. Wilson, *Víshṇu Purāṇa*, chap. 7.
11. Swami Madhavananda, *The Bṛihádāraṇyaka Upanishad, with the commentary of Shankaracharya* (Calcutta: Advaita Ashrama, 1965).
12. Roy, *Mahābhārata.*
13. M. Bernal, *Black Athena* (London: Vintage, 1987); J. McLeish, Number (London: Flamingo, 1992).
14. B. G. Tilak, *Orion* (Poona: Tilak Brothers, 1955).
15. S. B. Roy, *Prehistoric Lunar Astronomy* (New Delhi: Institute of Chronology, 1976).
16. J. P. Mallory, *In Search of the Indo-Europeans* (London: Thames & Hudson, 1991).
17. E. Hadingham, "The Mummies of Xin Jiang," *Discover* (April 1994): 68 ff.

## CHAPTER 1

1. Hereafter cited as RV. This and all subsequent translations are from R. T. H. Griffith, *The Hymns of the Ṛg Veda* (Varanasi: Chowkhamba Sanskrit Series, 1971).
2. For more on the A.svíns, see chapters 2 and 4.
3. For more on heliocentrism in the Vedas, see chapter 3.

## CHAPTER 2

1. A. C. Das, *Ṛg Vedic India* (Delhi: Motilal Banarsidass, 1971).
2. Z. A. Ragozin, *Vedic India* (Delhi: Munshiram Manohar Lal, 1961).
3. S. Kak, "On the Chronology of Ancient India," *Indian Journal of History of Sciences* 22, no. 3 (1987): 222 ff.
4. E. C. Krupp, ed., *In Search of Ancient Astronomies* (New York: Penguin, 1984).
5. Kak, "On the Chronology of Ancient India."
6. S. B. Roy, *Prehistoric Lunar Astronomy* (New Delhi: Institute of Chronology, 1976). Here is Yāska's commentary: "Vṛíka-

Vivṛita Jyotiśka va vikrita jyotiśka va vikrānta jyotiśka va," that is, "one whose brightness increases and decreases."

7. A. Koestler, *The Sleepwalkers* (London: Hutchinson, 1959).
8. B. G. Sidharth, "Ancient Indian Astronomy—A Surprise," *B. M. Birla Planetarium Report,* November 1985; paper presented at 91st IAU Colloquium on History of Oriental Astronomy, New Delhi, 1985.
9. It may be pointed out that the Ṡathápatha Brāhmaṇa declares that the Sun destroys the *rākṣasas* (demons), which are invoked in Vedic literature. The demons really represent darkness, a fact that is acknowledged at places by scholars. In the Purāṇas the Índra-Vṛitrá battle is a one-time encounter, whereas in the Ṛg Veda the battle takes place again and again.
10. B. G. Sidharth, "Ancient Indian Astronomy: A Metrical Code of Intercalation," *B. M. Birla Science Centre Report,* December 1990; paper presented at the National Symposium on Science and Technology in Ancient India, Hyderabad, 1990.
11. P. V. Holay, *Vedic Astronomy* (Nagpur: Shri Babasaheb Apte Smarak Samitee, 1989).
12. B. G. Tilak, *The Arctic Home in the Vedas* (Poona: Tilak Brothers, 1971).
13. B. G. Sidharth, "Ancient Indian Cosmology," *History of Indian Science and Technology,* vol. 2 (New Delhi: Sandeep Prakasan, 1990).
14. *The Śatapatha Brāhmaṇa,* vol. 12, (Delhi: Motilal Banarsidass, 1978).
15. S. B. Dikshit, *Bharatiya Jyotisha* (Calcutta: Govt. of India Press, 1969).
16. B. G. Sidharth, "Contributions to Scientific Thought: Ancient Hindus vs. the Greeks," *B. M. Birla Planetarium Report,* March 1989; talk given at the Silver Jubilee of the Indian Geophysical Union.
17. A. N. Whitehead, *Science and the Modern World* (Cambridge: Cambridge University Press, 1953).
18. The name Pythagoras can be traced to the Sanksrit Pita guru.

His ideas on music and cosmology are similar to those in ancient Indian tradition. He is also known to have been in the East. It would be interesting to investigate if he originally came from India.

## CHAPTER 3

1. B. G. Sidharth, "Glimpses of the Amazing Astronomy of the Ṛg Veda," *Indological Taurinensia* 6, (1978).
2. A. Hillebrandt, *Vedische Mythologie*, trans. S. R. Sarma, vol. 1 (Delhi: Motilal Banarsidass, 1981).

## CHAPTER 4

1. B. G. Sidharth, "The Secret Astronomy of the Hindus"; also, see chapter 2.
2. Ibid.
3. A. B. Keith, *Taittirīya Saṃhita* (Delhi: Motilal Banarsidass, 1967), (4.4.10).
4. See chapter 2.
5. A. A. Macdonell and A. B. Keith, *Vedic Index of Names and Subjects* (Delhi: Motilal Banarsidass, 1982).

## CHAPTER 5

1. B. G. Sidharth, "Ancient Hindu Cosmology"; paper presented at the fiftieth session of the Indian Society for the History of Mathematics, Jadavpur University, 1981. Also see *Journal of the Birla Planetarium* 4, no. 2 (1983).
2. C. Sagan, *Cosmos* (New York: Random House, 1980); C. Ronan *Deep Space*, (New York: Macmillan, 1982).
3. W. R. Drake, *Gods and Spacemen in the Ancient West* (New York: Signet Books, 1974), and E. von Däniken, *Chariots of the Gods?* (New York: G.P. Putnam's Sons, 1970).

4. P. Moore, *The History of Astronomy* (London: Macdonald & Company, 1983), p. 15.
5. M. Sarkar, and B. B. Dutta, *Astronomy* (Calcutta: Kamala Book Depot).
6. C. Dimmit and J. A. B. van Buitenen, *Classical Hindu Mythology* (Calcutta: Rupa, 1983).
7. B. G. Sidharth, "Glimpses of the Amazing Astronomy of the Ṛg Veda," *Indologica Taurinensia* 4 (1978).
8. See Dimmit and van Buitenen, *Classical Hindu Mythology*, for a brief summary.
9. See note 7.
10. "The Hymns of the Ṛg Veda," Vol. 1, The Chowkhamba Sanskrit Series, 1971 (translated by R. T. H. Griffith).
11. Sidharth, B. G., "Ancient Indian Astronomy: A Surprise"; paper presented at Colloquium 91 on History of Oriental Astronomy, International Astronomical Union, 1985. INSA, New Delhi. Also *B.M. Birla Planetarium Research Publication* BPRH/85.

## CHAPTER 6

1. See Dimmit and van Buitenen, *Classical Hindu Mythology*, for a review of these works.
2. Satya Prakash Saraswati, *The Critical and Cultural Study of the Śatapatha Brāhmaṇa* (New Delhi: Govindram Hasanand, 1988).
3. Dikshit, *Bharatiya Jyotisha Shastra*.
4. W. Durant, *Our Oriental Heritage* (New York: Simon & Schuster, 1954).
5. Dikshit, *Bharatiya Jyotisha Shastra*, and B. V. Subbarayappa, "India's Contribution to the History of Science," in *India's Contribution to World Thought and Culture* (Madras: Vivekananda Rock Memorial Committee, 1970), pp. 47 ff.
6. N. V. B. S. Dutt, "Manvantaras and Cyclic Tectonic Activity"; paper presented at All India Seminar on Ancient Indian

Astronomy, B.M. Birla Planetarium, Hyderabad, 1987.
7. C. N. Srinivasiengar, *The History of Ancient Indian Mathematics* (Calcutta: World Press, 1967); and G. R. Kaye, *Hindu Astronomy* (New Delhi: Cosmo Publications, 1981).
8. S. B. Roy, *Prehistoric Lunar Astronomy* (New Delhi: Institute of Chronology, 1976).
9. B. G. Sidharth, "Ancient Indian Cosmology," *History of Indian Science and Technology*, vol. 11 (New Delhi: Sandeep Prakasan, 1990). These verses were translated by the author.
10. *The Institute of Víshṇu* XX, 1–20, trans. by Julius Jolly (Oxford: Sacred Books of the East Series, Vol. VII, 1880).
11. Sagan, Cosmos, p. 195; Ronan, Deep Space, p. 146.
12. *The Insititute of Víshṇu*, 97.19.
13. See chapter 2.
14. Roy, *Mahābhārata.*
15. H. H. Wilson, *The Ṛg Veda Sanhita*, vol. 1, (New Delhi: Cosmo Publications, 1977).
16. See Tilak, *The Arctic Home in the Vedas*, and N. N. Law, *Age of the Ṛg Veda* (Calcutta: K. L. Mukhopadhyay, 1965).
17. Kak, "On the Chronology of Ancient India."
18. F. E. Pargiter, *Ancient Indian Historical Tradition* (Delhi: Motilal Banarsidass, 1997).
19. G. V. Tagore, *Kūrmá Purāṇa* (Delhi: Motilal Banarsidass, 1981).
20. R. Shama Shastry, *Gavam Ayana* (Madras: Wesleyan Mission Press, 1908).
21. A. Dahiquist, *Megasthenes and Indian Religion* (Delhi: Motilal Banarsidass, 1977).
22. S. B. Roy, *Ancient India* (New Delhi: Institute of Chronology, 1975); Pargiter, *Ancient Indian Historical Tradition.*
23. H. S. Spencer, *The Aryan Ecliptic Cycle* (Poona: H. P. Vasvani, 1965).
24. Ibid.
25. B. K. Thapar, "The Aryans: A Reappraisal of the Problems,"

in *India's Contribution of World Thought and Culture* (Madras: Vivekananda Rock Memorial Committee, 1970), p. 147 ff.

26. *Vanished Civilizations* (Sydney: Reader's Digest, 1988).
27. C. Renfrew, *Before Civilization* (London: Jonathan Cape, 1973; L. S. Stavrianos, *A Global History* (Englewood Cliffs, New Jersey: Prentice-Hall, 1983).
28. C. Renfrew, *Archaeology and Language: The Puzzle of Indo-European Origins* (London: Jonathan Cape, 1987).
29. *Secrets of the Past* (New York: Reader's Digest, 1980).
30. H. H. Hicks and R. N. Anderson, *Journal of Indo-European Studies* 18 (1990): 425–46.
31. A. Ghosh, *An Encyclopaedia of Indian Archaeology*, vol. 2, (New Delhi: Munshiram Manoharlal Publications, 1989).
32. Kak, "On the Chronology of Ancient India."
33. *Ancient Civilizations of the East and West* (Moscow: Progress Publishers, 1988).
34. *Der Spiegel*, 33 (1991): 160 ff.
35. For more on Nevali Cori, see chapter 8.
36. At the conclusion of my article "Is the Ṛg Vedic Civilization the Oldest?" (*B. M. Birla Science Centre Research Report* [Hyderabad] [August 1991]), which recapitulates the conclusions of this chapter, I suggested that the Ṛg Vedic seers were either the elite Anatolian class, or had contact with them, which points to the fact that the Ṛg Vedic civilization is the oldest in the world, and in any case, far ahead of its time.

    It would be well to remember that in earlier epochs the relative cultural development in different regions was far more unequal than in recent times when fast communication and, more recently, telecommunications have tended to bring in an even greater degree of homogeneity. Because of this fact, the rate of change and diffusion of culture and language were much slower when compared with modern times.

    Furthermore, considering the Sanskritic influence in the Anatolian region, not only from the above-suggested Ṛg

Vedic connection but the otherwise well-established presence of Sanskritic names of deities, places, and so on, and the Sanskritic influence in Indo-European languages (note that Antalaya was a part of Anatolia, and is probably the origin of the latter name; or the word *ārya*, which comes from the Sanskrit root *āri* "to plow"), it may be better to use the term Sanskritic rather than the standard Indo-European (cf. P. N. Oak, *World Vedic Heritage* [New Delhi: Institute for Rewriting Indian History, 1984] for some interesting views). In suggesting this, I am keeping in view historical reversals alluded to above, as against a generally accepted linear view of history, which traces Sanskrit back to an older Indo-European ancestor language.

## Chapter 7

1. See also my "Mahāyugá: The Great Cosmic Cycle and the Date of the Ṛg Veda," *B. M. Birla Science Centre Research Report* (Hyderabad), (February 1991), and "Is the Ṛg Vedic Civilization the Oldest?," *B. M. Birla Science Centre Research Report* (Hyderabad) (August 1991).
2. See A. B. Keith, trans., *Taittirīya Saṃhita*, and the *Taittirīya Brāhmaṇa*.
3. *Mahābhārata*, Adi Parva trans. P. C. Roy (Calcutta: Oriental Publishing Co., 1963).

   Nowhere in the Ṛg Veda can Bṛhaspati be identified with the planet Jupiter. On the contrary, the identification of Bṛhaspati with Agní or the Sun is quite evident. For example, Bṛhaspati, like Agní or Sūrya, the Sun, has seven mouths, or seven rays, and drives away darkness (cf. RV 2.23 or 4.50).
4. See chapter 2 and my "Glimpses of the Amazing Astronomy of the Ṛg Veda."
5. Dikshit, *Bharatiya Jyotiśha Shastra*.
6. Hillebrandt, *Vedic Mythology*, vol 2: 100.

7. See chapter 6.
8. Dikshit, *Bharatiya Jyotiśha Shastra.*
9. Hillebrandt, *Vedic Mythology*, vol. 2: 123.
10. K. D. Abhyankar, "Antiquity of the Vedic Calendar"; paper presented at the International Symposium on Indian and Other Asiatic Astronomies, Hyderabad, 1991.
11. S. R. Rao, *Excavation of Submerged Ports-Dwarka, a Case Study* (Goa: Proceedings of the First Indian Conference on Marine Archaeology of Indian Ocean Countries, National Institute of Oceanography, 1988).
12. H. H. Hicks and R. N. Anderson, *Journal of Indo-European Studies* 18 (1990): 425–46.
13. D. Anthony, D. Y. Telegin, and D. Brown, "The Origin of Horseback Riding," *Vigyan* (*Scientific American*, Indian Edition) (January 1992).

## CHAPTER 8

1. *Der Spiegel*, 33, (1991): 160 ff.
2. J. E. Schwartzberg, *A Historical Atlas of South Asia* (Chicago: The University of Chicago Press, 1978).
3. See chapters 6 and 10; also B. G. Sidharth, "Mahāyugá: The Great Cosmic Cycle and the Date of the Ṛg Veda"; "Is the Ṛg Vedic Civilization the Oldest?"; "Antiquity of the Ṛg Veda," *International Symposium on Indian and Other Asiatic Astronomies*, Hyderabad, 1991, in press.
4. D. Frawley, *Gods, Sages and Kings: Vedic Secrets of Ancient Civilization* (Salt Lake City: Passage Press, 1991), pp. 165 ff.; K. D. Abhyankar, "Antiquity of the Vedic Calendar" (Hyderabad: *Proceedings of the International Symposium on Indian & Other Asiatic Astronomies*, 1991).
5. C. Renfrew, *Archaeology and Language.*
6. J. Kurdo, *Kurdistan* (London: Kurdish Cultural Centre, 1988), p. 50.

7. T. T. Sanefur, *Discrete Dyanamical Systems* (Oxford: Clarenden Press, 1990).
8. R. C. Majumdar, *Ancient India* (Varanasi: Motilal Banarsidass, 1952).
9. R. Pandey, *Hindu Sanskar* (Varanasi: Chowkhamba Publishing House, 1957).
10. R. K. Mukherjee, *Hindu Civilization* (Bombay: Bharatiya Vidya Bhavan, 1977).
11. Anthony, Telegin, and Brown, "The Origin of Horseback Riding."
12. Kak, "On the Chronology of Ancient India"; cf. chapter 1.
13. H. S. Spencer, *Are the Gathas Pre-Vedic?* (Poona: H. P. Vaswani, 1965), p. 11 ff.
14. Kurdo, *Kurdistan*, p. 5 ff.
15. A. Parpola, "The Coming of the Aryans to Iran and India," *Studia Orientalia* (Helsinki) no. 64, (1988): 192–305.
16. Spencer, *Are the Gathas Pre-Vedic?*, p. 6.

## CHAPTER 9

1. Stavrianos, *A Global History*, p. 25 ff.
2. R. C. Mazumdar, *Ancient India* (Delhi: Motilal Banarsidass, 1991), p. 28 ff.
3. V. Illingworth, *A Dictionary of Astronomy* (London: Pan Books, 1981).
4. Macdonell and Keith, *Vedic Index of Names and Subjects* (Delhi: Motilal Banarsidass, 1982), p. 409 ff.
5. S. B. Roy, *Ancient India*, p. 66.
6. *Statesman* (Calcutta), October 30, 1979.
7. J. Eggeling, *The Śatapatha Brāhmaṇa.*
8. M. Haug, trans., *Aitereya Brāhmaṇam of the Ṛg Veda*, vol. 2, (Varanasi: Bharatiya Publishing House, 1977), p. 173 ff, p. 212 ff.
9. Gambirananda, *Eight Upanishads* (Calcutta: Advaita Ashrama, 1978).

10. See chapter 1 and Sidharth, "Glimpses of the Amazing Astronomy of the Ṛg Veda"; "The Unmythical Purāṇas: A Study in Reverse Symbolism"; and "Did Indians Pioneer Astronomy?"
11. Dikshit, *Bharatiya Jyotiśha Shastra.*
12. Tilak, *Orion*, p. 215 ff.
13. See chapter 8.
14. J. E. Schwartzberg, ed. *A Historical Atlas of South Asia* (Chicago: The University of Chicago Press, 1978).
15. C. L. Redman, *The Rise of Civilization* (San Francisco: W. H. Freeman, 1978).
16. H. Hauptmann, "Nevali Cori," *Nürnberger Blätter Zur Archaologie* (1991–92): 15 ff.
17. J. F. Jarrige and R. H. Meadow, "The Antecedents of Civilization in the Indus Valley," *Scientific American* 243 (1980): 102 ff.
18. Schwartzberg, *Historical Atlas of South Asia.*
19. S. R. Rao, *Dawn and Devolution of the Indus Civilization* (New Delhi: Āditya Prakashan, 1991), pp. 272–281.
20. S. C. Kak, "The Indus Tradition and Indo-Aryans," *Mankind Quarterly*, 32 no. 3 (1992) p. 43; S. Hajra, *On the Decipherment of the Inscriptions of the Seals of Harappa and Mohenjadaro* (Calcutta: Subarnarekha, 1974).
21. Parpola, "The Coming of the Aryans to Iran and India," pp. 192–305.
22. S. Piggott, *Prehistoric India* (Middlesex: Penguin, 1961); Kak, "On the Chronology of Ancient India."
23. See chapter 8 and Sidharth, "A Lost Anatolian Civilization—Is it Vedic?"
24. Rao, *Excavation of Submerged Ports-Dwaraka, a Case Study.*
25. Rao, *Dawn and Devolution of the Indus Civilization*, pp. 272–81; A. D. Pusalker, *Studies in Epics and Purāṇas of India* (Bombay: Bharatiya Vidya Bhavan, 1955), p. 75 ff.
26. Roy, *The Mahābhārata.*
27. Schwartzberg, *Historical Atlas of South Asia.*
28. J. G. Shaffer, "The Indo-Aryan invasions: Cultural Myth and

Archaeological Reality," in *The People of South Asia*, J. R. Lukacs, ed. (New York: Plenum, 1984).

29. See chapters 6 and 7; Sidharth, "The Antiquity of the Ṛg Veda"; Frawley, *Gods, Sages and Kings*, p. 165 ff.
30. Parpola, "The Coming of the Aryans to Iran and India," pp. 195–302.
31. See chapter 5.
32. See chapter 7.
33. B. S. Dehiya, "Aryan Tribes in West Asia," *Vishveshvaranand Indological Journal*, 36 (1988): 219.
34. Parpola, "The Coming of the Aryans to Iran and India," pp. 195–302.
35. Ibid.
36. D. Bongard-Levin and A. Viogasin, *The Image of India* (Moscow: Progress Publishers, 1984), p. 190.
37. Ibid.
38. Ibid.
39. L. L. Cavali-Sforza, "Genes, Peoples and Languages," *Vigyan (Scientific American*, Indian Edition*)*, December (1991): p. 70 ff.
40. Renfrew, "*Archaeology and Language*."
41. FACETS (Embassy of France in India), no.1 (1992): 24 ff, gives a quick summary.
42. Parpola, "The Coming of the Aryans to Iran and India," pp. 195–302.
43. G. Thibaut and S. Dvivedi, trans., *Panchasiddhantika of Varaha Mihira* (Lahore: Motilal Banarsidass, 1930), p. 19.
44. Bougard-Levin and Viogasin, *The Image of India*, p. 19 ff.
45. W. J. Wilkins, *Hindu Mythology* (Calcutta: Rupa, 1988), p. 15 ff.
46. A historical find, near Nevali Cori has just been reported by Dr. Gillian Vogelsang-Eastwood of the National Museum of Ethnology in Leiden, Prof. Robert Braidwood of the University of Chicago, and Prof. Frank Hole of Yale University. This is a small piece of cloth found at Cayonu, dating back to 8000 B.C. (According to current ideas cloth weaving would go back to

around 3500 B.C.) This dramatic find fits in very harmoniously with the date, culture, and location of the Ṛg Vedic civilization, as proposed in this paper.

47. D. A. Mackenzie, *Myths and Legends: India* (London: Bracken Books, 1986), p. 19.
48. A. de. Riencourt, *The Eye of Shiva* (Condor: Souvenir Press, 1982).
49. B. S. Dehiya, "Aryan Tribes in West Africa," *Vishveswaran and Indological Journal*, vol. 26 (1988): 219.

## CHAPTER 10

1. See chapter 6; also Sidharth, "Mahāyugá: The Great Cosmic Cycle and the Date of the Ṛg Veda."
2. See chapter 5.
3. Ibid.
4. H. H. Wilson ed., *The Víshṇu Purāṇa* ( Calcutta: Punthi Pustak, 1979), p. 192.
5. Dimmit and van Buitenen, *Classical Hindu Mythology*, p. 92.
6. "Ādityahrdayam" (Madras: Sri Ramakrishna Math, 1993), p. 12.
7. See chapter 7; also Sidharth, "Antiquity of the Ṛg Veda."
8. Macdonell, *Vedic Mythology*, p. 145.
9. Dimmit and van Buitenen, *Classical Hindu Mythology*, p. 310 ff.
10. Pargiter, *Mārkaṇḍeya Purāṇa*, chapter p. 459.
11. Wilson, *The Víshṇu Purāṇa*, chapter 11, p. 192 ff.
12. See chapter 7.
13. R. T. H. Giffith, trans., *The Hymns of the Ṛg Veda* (Varanasi, 1971), pp. 1–164.
14. Wilson, *The Víshṇu Purāṇa*, p. 192 ff.
15. Swami Tapasyananda, trans., *Sri Visṇu Sahasranama* (Madras: Sri Ramakrishna Math, 1971), p. 41 ff.
16. Dimmit and van Buitenen, *Classical Hindu Mythology*, p. 320.
17. See chapter 6.
18. Ibid.

# CHAPTER 11

1. Pusalker, *Studies in Epics and Purāṇas of India*, p. 75 ff; N. V. R. Krishnamacharya, *The Mahābhārata* (Tirupati: Tirumala Tirupati Devasthanams, 1983).
2. S. B. Roy, *Ancient India*, p. 36 ff.
3. Thibaut and Dvivedi, *The Pañcasiddhantika of Varaha Mihira*, p. 79 ff.
4. P. V. Holay, *Vedic Astronomy* (*Vedaanga Jyotisha*) (Nagpur: Babasaheb Apte Smarak Samitee,1989), p. 105.
5. G. R. Kay, *Hindu Astronomy* (New Delhi: Cosmo Publications, 1981), p. 14 ff.
6. W. Jones, *Asiatic Researches*, vol. 2 (New Delhi: Cosmo Publicatons, 1979), p. 88 ff.
7. J. Bentley, *A Historical View of the Hindu Astronomy* (New Delhi: Cosmo Publications, 1981), p. 67 ff.
8. K. Mukherjee, *Popular Hindu Astronomy* (Calcutta: Saraswaty Press Ltd., 1969), pp. 48–53.
9. Ibid.
10. H. Mucke and J. Meeus, *Canon of Solar Eclipses* (Vienna: Astronomisches Buro, 1992), p. 325.
11. This total solar eclipse was seen nearer sunset at a slightly higher latitude in the adjoining parts of China. In this context, and in the context of the Indo-European Tocharians of Chinese Turkistan, it is remarkable that recent excavations in nearby parts of China have unearthed an Indo-European settlement going back to the second millennium B.C.!
12. Wilson, *Víshṇu Purāṇa*, p. 389.
13. F. Wilford, *Asiatic Researches*, vol. 5 (New Delhi: Cosmo Publications, 1979), p. 241 ff.
14. A. Foucher, *Notes on the Ancient Geography of Gandhara* (Varanasi: Bhartiya Publishing House, 1974), p. 5.
15. It is interesting to note that the Mahābhārata battle took place at Samantapañcaka, an ancient site with five pools of blood, according to Paraśurāma. This could well be the Pañcatirtha

near Peshawar, a site with five holy tanks, visited by the Pāṇḍavas.

16. Parpola, "The Coming of the Aryans to Iran and India."
17. S. R. Rao, *Dawn and Devolution of the Indus Civilization*, pp. 272–81.
18. S. Jagannathan and N. Krishna, *Ganesha, the Auspicious . . . the Beginning* (Bombay: Vakil, Feffer and Simons, 1992), p. 33.
19. Piggott, *Prehistoric India.*

## CHAPTER 12

1. See chapters 6, 7, and 9.
2. See chapter 9.
3. See chapters 5 and 10; also Santillana and von Dechend, *Hamlet's Mill.*
4. Haug, *Aitareya Brāhmaṇam of the Ṛg Veda*, vol. 2, p. 200; Griffith, *The Hymns of the Ṛg Veda*, p. 611.
5. See chapters 7 and 9 for why Róhiṇī is at the winter solstice and not the vernal equinox.
6. See chapter 9 and references.
7. Pusalker, *Studies in Epics and Purāṇas of India*, p. 174 ff.
8. See chapter 5.
9. See chapters 7 and 9.
10. Hauptmann, "Nevali Cori."
11. See chapter 9.
12. Krishnamacharya, *The Mahābhārata.*
13. See chapter 7.
14. See chapter 11.
15. Parpola, "The Coming of the Aryans to Iran and India."

## CHAPTER 13

1. Rao, *Dawn and Devolution of the Indus Civilization*, pp. 272–81.
2. A. K. Bag, *Science and Civilization in India (Harappan Period)* (New Delhi: Navrang, 1985), p. 98 ff.

3. Bongard-Levin and Vigasin, *The Image of India*, p. 194.
4. Haug, *Aitareya Brāhmaṇam of the Ṛg Veda*, 4.17; R. T. H. Griffith, *The Hymns of the Atharva Veda*, vol. 2, (Varanasi: The Chowkhamba Sanskrit Series, 1965), 12.3.41; S. S. Apte, *Vedic Astronomy and Mythology* (Pune: Gokul Masik Prakasan, 1978), p. 69.
5. D. K. Roy and I. Devi, *Kumbhá* (Bombay: Bharatiya Vidya Bhavan, 1955).
6. P. Gangooly, ed., *The Surya Siddhānta* (Delhi: Motilal Banarsidass, 1989); K. S. Shukla, trans., *Aryabhatiya* (New Delhi: Indian National Science Academy, 1976).
7. V. N. Misra, "Lost Sárasvatī: The Cradle of Harappan Civilization," *Manthan*, October 1994–March 1995; B. Ghose, A. Kar, and Z. Hussain, "The Last Courses of the Sárasvatī River in the Great Indian Desert: New Evidence from Lands at Imagery," *Itihas Darpan*, vol. 3, nos. 1 and 2 (1995).
8. See chapters 7 and 9.
9. Ibid.
10. N. V. R. Krishnamacharya, *The Mahābhārata* (Tirupati: TTD, 1983).
11. Swami Satyaprakasa Sárasvatī, *Founders of Sciences in Ancient India*, vol. 1 (Delhi: Govindram Hasanand, 1986).
12. Roy, *The Mahābhārata* (Vana Parva).
13. Bongard-Levin and Vigasin.
14. H. Zimmer, *Myths and Symbols in Indian Art and Civilization* (Delhi: Motilal Banarsidass,1990), p. 52.
15. S. Jagannathan and N. Krishna, *Ganesha* (Bombay: Vakils, Feffer & Simmons, 1992), p. 34.
16. See chapter 11.
17. Jagannathan and Krishna, *Ganesha*, p. 33.
18. R. B. Pandey, *Indian Palaeography*, part 1 (Varanasi: Motilal Banarsidass, 1957), p. 30 ff.

*Sculpture of Brahma in his triple aspect or Trimūrti: Brahma the creator, Víshṇu the preserver, and Śiva the destroyer.*

*Sculpture of Sūrya, the Sun, with the wheel of time or the Sudarśana cakra in his hand.*

*Sculpture of Kārttikeya from Kṛíttikā or Pleiades.*

*Sculpture of Vīrabhadra, a monster created by Śiva to destroy the sacrifice of Dáksa, related to the omission of the nákshatra or star Abhijit or Vega.*

Photos: Birla Archaeological and Cultural Research Institute

Birla Archaeological and Cultural Research Institute

*Sculpture of Padmanābha, the reclining Viṣṇu with the lotus Earth sprouting from his navel.*

Birla Archaeological and Cultural Research Institute

*Sculpture of Naṭrāja, literally "the king of dance," symbolizing Śiva's rhythmic cosmic dance of destruction.*

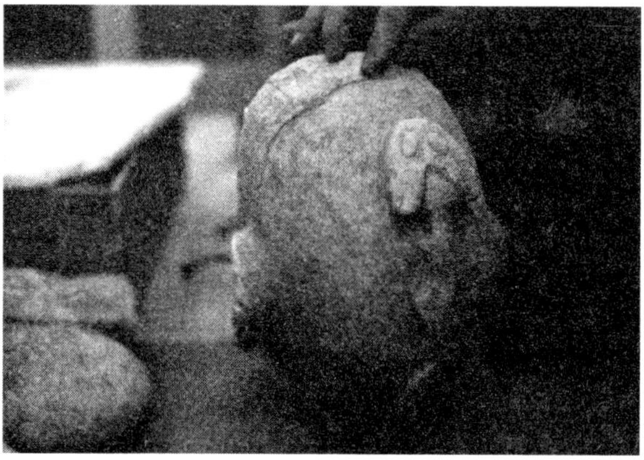

B. G. Sidharth

*Sculpture of a shaven head with a pigtail-like tuft of hair (circa 7,500 B.C. in Anatolia) that can be identified with a Vedic priest.*

Photos: Birla Archaeological and Cultural Research Institute

*Sculpture of the lion-borne Mother Goddess destroying evil.*

*Sculpture of the Trípurá myth*

*An early depiction of the Samudra Manthana legend (churning of the ocean) from Angkor wat.*

*A moment from the Kumbha Melā festival held once every twelve (and six) years—the oldest continuing religious congregation in the world.*

# INDEX

Aap 82
Abhijit (Vega) 159
Abhyankar 75
Aborigines 24, 106
Abraham 107
Acala 113
Achaeans 121
Ácyuta 113
Adhṛtah 115
Ādiśesha 10, 55
Áditi 31, 91, 119, 120, 129
Āditya 19
Āditya Hṛídayaṁ 5, 33, 112, 113
Afghanistan 94, 95, 99, 101, 117, 120, 121, 122, 123, 124
Agástya 17, 118, 127
Agha 74
Agní 32, 72, 88, 112, 126, 129, 133, 134
Agriculture 7, 67, 88, 92, 106
Ahah-Saṃvatsara 113
Ahhijava 121
Aitreya Brāhmaṇa 4, 5, 29, 74, 89, 91, 100, 107, 125, 129, 133, 135
Ajá-ékapada 74, 91
Akaivasa 121
Alberuni 135
Aldebaran 125, 129, 135
Alexander 1, 16
Alexandria 104
Allahabad 132
Alpha arietes 72, 75, 130
Alpha Draconis 65
Altyn Depe 94, 95
Amaurey de Reincourt 107
Ambar 82
Amṛíta 132
Anantá 55, 110
Anatolia 8, 9, 67, 71, 75, 77, 81, 92, 93, 96, 103, 121, 128, 160
Anatolian 79, 104, 106
Ancient chronology 3
Ancient civilization 94
Ancient science 3
Áṅgirasá 132, 134
Angkor wat 161
Annual motion 55, 74
Annual orbit 55
Annual parallax 48
Áṉśa 47
Antares 74, 115
Arab 35, 38, 87, 88
Āraṇyakas 23
Archaeologists 79, 80, 99
Archimedes 38, 39
Arctic 66
Aries 48, 127
Aristarchus 39, 99
Aristotle 36
Árjuna 62, 63, 119, 120
Arudra 135
Arya 107

Ā́ryabhaṭṭa 35, 37, 133
Aryan 17, 96, 102, 106, 121, 122; god, 75; invasion 23, 91, 97, 99; tribes, 75, 96
Aryans 64, 67, 68, 99, 100
Ashivyayantau viváshvatah 48
Ashur 17
Aśokan edicts 37
Asterism 66, 91, 129
Astrologers 19
Astrology 16, 34
Astro-myth 4
Astronaut 52
Astronomers 19, 26, 29, 33, 49, 53
Astronomy 1, 2, 3, 4, 7, 15, 17, 30, 34, 38, 61, 63, 91, 107, 129
Asuras 91, 99, 100, 109, 110, 112, 127
Aśvín 19, 48
Aśvinī nakshatra 9, 49
Aswathama 131
Aswini 48, 72, 127, 130
Aswins 2, 9, 17, 18, 26, 27, 37, 40, 46, 47, 49, 51, 56, 72, 88, 127, 128
Atharva Veda 28, 46, 80, 87
Atlantis 76
Atmosphere 27, 45, 51, 56
Átri 72, 112
Auroch 134
Auroral displays 18
Āvartana 114
Avesta 24, 67, 83, 123
Avestan 82, 98; Avestan literature, 29
Ayodhyā 126
Āyurvedic 81

Babylonia 15, 16, 35
Babylonian 17, 19, 24, 90; astronomy, 104
Bactria 99, 100, 103, 122
Bactrian plain 94
Bahrain 95
Bali 54, 110
Baluchistan 93, 94, 103
Beta Arietes 72, 75, 130
Betelgeuse 135
Bhagavad Gītā 33, 62, 64
Bhāgavata 59
Bhāravṛitta 114
Bhīshma 104, 113, 118, 119, 120, 129
Bhujyai 47
Bhūtâdi 113
Bhuvanani 48
Big bang 63
Bihar 79
Boghuz Koi 23, 82, 96, 99, 121
Bopp 107
Brahma 12, 57, 62, 63, 64, 136, 159
Brahma's day 33
Brahmaguptad 37
Brāhmaṇas 4, 23, 29, 59, 74, 91, 104, 107, 109, 126, 127, 129, 133
Brahmâṇḍa 81
Brāhmaṇic 81, 134
Brāhmin 17, 102
Brāhmin city 103
Brāhmi script 135
Brick altars 94
Bṛíhaspáti 64, 72, 127
Bronze age 95, 122

Cakrá 111
Calendar 25, 30, 85, 86, 87, 117, 133
Cancer 57, 61
Caṇḍála 126
Candramauli 55
Canopus 118
Canx 121
Caspian Sea 95, 122
Caste system 82
Castor 26, 91, 129
Catal Huyuk 67, 68, 135
Caucasian 97, 103
Celestial 72; great age, 61; sphere, 42
Celtic 107
Central Asia 94, 103, 106, 121
Chakrâvaka 47
Chalcolithic 68
Chaldean 10; saros, 61
Chandramshuh 114
China 11, 34, 87, 88, 120, 121, 123
Christian 82; era, 35, 61, 117
Chronology 2, 7, 8, 68, 98
Citra 135
Citrá Sikhaṇḍi 119

Civilization 75, 77; Harappan 85
Clay tablets 16, 20, 23
Comets 36
Constellations 28, 33, 42, 57, 62, 126, 132
Copernicus 17, 34, 36, 37, 38, 39, 42, 49
Cosmic Cycle, The Great, 7
Cosmology 64
Cosmos 55, 56, 57
Crescent 55; moon, 88
Crystal sphere(s), 36, 37
Cynthia, as moon, 26

Dahae 24, 98
Daitya 56
Dáksha 53, 54, 56, 112, 159
Dark Age 95
Darkness 27, 51, 53, 54
Dāsas 23, 24, 98, 99, 100, 106
Dashly III 95, 96, 99, 101, 122
Dásyus 23, 24, 98, 99, 100
Dawn 28, 55
Day 31, 53, 60, 63, 90, 109, 111, 113; light, 29, 30
Dechend, Iterthe von, 4
Decimal: system, 36; enumeration, 37
Declination, the Sun's, 72, 74, 126
Deity(ies), 46, 71, 85, 101, 103
Delhi 94, 95
Delphinus. *See* Dhánishṭha 118
Delta Cancri 62, 65, 71, 72, 127
Demigods 26
Demons 51, 54, 55, 88, 127
Devas 42, 88, 89, 91, 109, 110, 127, 132
Deváyāna 8
Dhánishṭha 118, 120
Dharaṇī Dharāḥ 114
Dhárma Sūtras 81
Dhruvá 113
Digambara 40, 55
Dikarin 55
Dikshit 73, 91
Directions, the four, 55
Diurnal motion 72, 74
Domestication of animals 92
Dravidian 95, 97, 102, 103, 122
Dumezil 104
Durgā 103, 122, 135
Dvāpara Yugá 60, 66, 127, 129, 130
Dvārakā 75, 97, 123
Dvevartana 122
Dwarf 113. *See* Vāman
Dyaus 40, 121

Earth 4, 5, 9, 10, 16, 17, 18, 19, 29, 31, 35, 36, 37, 39, 42, 45, 46, 49, 51, 52, 53, 54, 55, 56, 57, 66, 92, 106, 110, 111, 112, 113, 114, 115, 160
Eclipse 10, 11, 29, 35, 61, 62, 90, 112
Egypt 7, 16, 35, 67, 85, 92, 93
Egyptian 34, 86, 121
Eighth millennium 104
Ékavaṛtana 122
Elamite God, 107
Elliptical 36
Epic 119
Epipaleolithic 92, 106, 127
Epoch 127, 129
Equinox 10, 32, 110
Euphrates 78
Europe 15, 34, 35, 36, 38, 104
European invasion 97
Evening star 15, 16, 18, 26, 27, 35

Fire altars 97, 99, 101
Fourth millennium 85
Full moon 30, 86, 88

Galileo 26
Gaṇas 135
Gandhāras 120, 121
Gandharva 89, 90
Gaṇêśa 119, 123, 135
Gáṅgā 119
Ganges 56
Garuḍa 103
Gautamá 83
Gāyatrī 17, 26, 31, 32, 90
Gharmā 47
Godavari valley 94
Goddess 103, 122
Gods 32, 35, 52, 54, 55, 60, 88, 89, 127

Gottochronology 104
Gravitational force 55, 110, 111
Great age 33, 62
Great Bear 101
Greco-Babylonian 1
Greek 1, 10, 15, 16, 17, 18, 19, 20, 32, 34, 36, 37, 38, 49, 83, 107
Gṛhya sutras 65
Gujarat 94, 95
Gupta script 88
Gurgan plain 95, 104, 122, 123

Halāhala 56
Hapta-hendus 24, 98
Harappan civilization 24, 68, 85, 92, 94, 95, 96, 97, 100, 101, 102, 103, 105, 107, 122, 134
Haraquaiti 98
Haridwar 132
Hásta 47, 118
Hattush 23
Heaven 18, 34, 52
Heidelberg 8
Heliocentric 18, 19, 25, 36, 37, 39, 41, 45, 46, 47, 49, 51, 57, 63, 111
Herakleides 39
Herald Hauptmann 8, 68, 77, 78, 79, 93
Hesiod 20
Hesperos 10
Himalaya 21
Hinduism 17, 20, 23, 33, 34, 35, 36, 38, 51, 52, 53, 61, 62, 63, 64, 66, 89, 96, 103, 105, 107, 136
Hipparchus 16, 19, 36, 37
Hittites 20, 23, 24, 82, 96, 102, 121, 122
Horse 9, 30, 53, 102
Hurrites 82

Ice age 7, 67, 71, 79, 92
Iconographic motifs 96
Iksvaku 66, 128
India 15, 16, 53, 79, 95, 97, 98
Indian subcontinent 64, 85, 93, 95
Indo-Aryan 7, 80, 81, 82, 85, 92, 95, 96, 97, 98, 100, 103, 104, 105, 122
Indo-European 7, 11, 23, 62, 64, 67, 82, 85, 104, 107, 121
Indo-Germanic 107
Índra 20, 27, 28, 29, 30, 45, 46, 51, 52, 54, 56, 73, 74, 75, 96, 109, 110, 115, 120, 126
Indra-Vṛitrá 110
Indus civilization 130, 132, 134, 135, 136
Indus seals 97, 98, 129, 133
Indus valley 68, 79, 85, 94, 105, 117, 121, 122, 123
Intercalary days 88
Intercalary month 31, 32, 89, 90
Intercalation 82
Iran, 24, 94, 95, 103, 117, 121, 122, 123; Greater, 96, 99, 100, 103, 105, 129
Iraq 82
Iron age 95
Isaac Newton 37
Itihâsa 4

Jaiminīya Brāhmaṇa 90
Janaka 20, 128
Janmejaya 121
Jayadratha 120
Jovian cycle 132, 133, 134
Judeo-Christian 107
Jupiter 64, 72, 132
Jyéshṭha 47, 74, 115, 126
Jyotisha 119
Jyotisha Vedāṅga 17, 87, 105, 117, 118, 125, 129

Kabul 120
Kāla 114
Kalhana 121
Kalibangan 94, 100, 101, 103, 122
Kali Yugá 60, 66, 129, 130, 133
Kalpa 33, 62
Kamboja 105, 120
Kanka 38
Kāṅkshá 121
Kantara 78
Kapi 113, 114

Kārttikeya 73, 101, 112, 126, 159
Kashmir 117, 120, 121
Kashmiri 82
Kassites 20, 82, 96
Kaurava 119
Kepler 17, 34, 36, 42, 49
Ketu 112
Kikkuli 82, 96, 122
King Vena 106
Kotdiji 94
Kṛishṇá 62, 75, 97, 123, 129
Kṛishṇá Yajur Veda 31
Kṛita Yugá 60, 66
Kṛíttikā 59, 65, 73, 91, 92, 101, 112, 129, 130, 133, 134, 159
Kumbhá Melā 132, 162
Kumbhá Rāśi 132
Kurds 82
Kūrmá 54, 55, 110, 111
Kūrmá Purāṇa 65, 66
Kúrukshetrá 124
Kūṭas 119

Latitude 11, 31, 118
Leo 135
Libra 73
Liṅga 96, 133, 135
Lokādhiṣthānam 115
Lotus 112, 160
Lunar asterism 48, 52, 62, 64, 65, 66, 67, 71, 72, 74, 87, 90, 101, 112, 118 125, 133
Lunar calendar 86; fortnight 88; month 19, 30, 32, 88; year 30, 31, 32, 88, 89
Luni-solar calendar 82, 86

Magha 74, 119, 120
Mahābhārata 2, 4, 5, 6, 11, 12, 28, 33, 34, 40, 48, 53, 59, 60, 62, 63, 72, 73, 75, 97, 98, 101, 102, 105, 112, 113, 117, 118, 120, 121, 123, 124, 127, 129, 130, 131, 134
Mahākalpa 63
Maharashtra 95
Mahāyugá 7, 11, 60, 62, 64, 65, 66, 90
Mahidharah 114
Maitrī Upanishad 61, 65
Mamalleswar temples 121
Mandara mount 54
Maṇí 131
Mantra 5
Marine archaeology 97, 123
Mārkaṇḍeya 6, 33, 59, 61, 63, 73, 112, 134
Mārtāṇḍa 119, 121
Mátsya Avatar 111
Mátsya Purāṇa 56
Medes 82
Megalithic 8, 77, 93, 128
Megasthenes 66, 128
Mehrgarh 9, 93, 94, 95, 100, 104, 131, 134
Mercury 15, 16, 18, 19, 26, 27, 35, 40, 41, 46, 47, 48, 51, 56, 72
Meshá 48
Mesopotamia 24, 67
Meton 32
Metonic cycle 32, 90
Mina 98
Mitani 20, 24, 96, 122
Mitra 20
Mohenjodaro 94, 131
Moon 5, 10, 15, 25, 26, 30, 35, 36, 45, 41, 46, 47, 48, 49, 54, 55, 56, 57, 61, 63, 65, 66, 86, 87, 90, 108, 110, 111, 112, 114, 133
Morning star 15, 16, 18, 26, 27, 28, 35
Mother earth 135
Mother goddess 105, 131, 135, 161; motifs, 123
Mriga 126
Mṛtyu 91
Muhūrtá 118
Müller, Max 7, 64, 104, 107

Nákshatra 10, 25, 30, 47, 49, 52, 53, 54, 56, 71, 72, 73, 84, 87, 88, 89, 90, 91, 108, 111, 112, 118, 120, 123, 133, 134, 135
Nalanda 79
Namazga V 95, 122
Nanda 120

Nandi 135
Nārāyaṇi Sena 119
Nāsatya 20, 96
Nasik 132
Naṭrāja 160
Neolithic 7, 77, 79, 106, 128
Nevalī Cori 8, 68, 69, 71, 77, 78, 79, 80, 81, 83, 93, 96, 100, 103, 104, 128, 129
Nīlakaṇṭha 55, 56
Nílamat Purāṇa 121
North Pole 31, 60, 66, 72, 74

Orbits 36, 52
Orion 9, 126, 135
Oscillating universe 6, 52, 63

Pāda 31, 47, 48
Padma 9
Padmanābha 9, 111, 160
Pahlavas 121
Paitāmaha Siddhānta 105, 117, 118
Pañcâṅga 30, 31
Pañcatīrtha 121
Pāṇḍavas 121, 131
Parallax 42, 46
Parāśara 117, 118
Pariksit 119, 120, 121
Parpola 82, 95, 99, 100, 129, 134
Pārtha 63
Particle physics 64
Paśúpáti 94, 97, 133
Patāñjali 65
Persian 20, 67, 82
Peshawar 120
Phalgunī 74, 119
Phallus 96, 133, 135
Philolaus 38, 39, 40
Pigtail 79, 160
Pillars 53, 55, 78
Pipal leaves 98, 131, 134
Pisces 134
Pitṛís 59
Planets 10, 15, 16, 18, 35, 114, 127; revolution, 33
Plato 36, 39, 76
Pleiades 59, 73, 91, 92, 101, 102, 129, 130, 133, 134, 159
Plutarch 39
Polar region 54
Pole star 16, 36, 61, 65
Pollux 26, 91, 129
Pottery 67, 93, 94, 95, 100, 103
Prajāpati 74, 90, 125, 126, 128, 133, 135
Precession 10, 19, 25, 32, 33, 36, 37, 61, 62
Priestly class 128
Priests 53, 131
Ptolemy 36
Púnarvasu 91, 129
Purāṇas 2, 3, 4, 5, 11, 12, 33, 51, 52, 53, 54, 55, 56, 57, 59, 60, 62, 66, 73, 81, 106, 109, 110, 111, 113, 115, 131, 132, 133, 134, 135, 136
Purva Bhádrapada 74, 91
Púshya 57, 61, 62, 64, 65, 67, 72, 73, 127
Pythagoras 16, 35, 39

Rāhú 112
Rākshasa 54
Rāma 126, 127, 128
Rāmāyaṇa 4, 5, 52, 55, 98, 112, 113, 126, 127, 128, 129, 130
Rao, S.R. 75, 95, 97, 101, 123
Rāśis 52
Ravi 113, 114
Regulus 74, 119
Renfrew, Colin, 67, 80, 104
Retrograde 18, 26
Revatī 134
Ṛg Veda 2, 7, 12, 17, 18, 19, 20, 23, 24, 26, 27, 32, 34, 36, 37, 39, 40, 42, 43, 45, 46, 47, 48, 49, 51, 52, 53, 54, 55, 56, 57, 62, 64, 65, 66, 67, 72, 73, 74, 76, 79, 80, 81, 82, 85, 86, 87, 89, 90, 91, 92, 97, 98, 99, 101, 103, 104, 106, 107, 113, 119
Ṛibhus 27, 29, 30, 49
Róhiṇī 73, 74, 118, 125, 126, 129, 134, 135
Romans 16, 36, 37

Rotation 5, 10, 54, 55, 56, 57
Rudra 31, 32, 64, 65, 135
Russia 99, 104

Sahasranāma 114
Samudra manthana 161
Saṅkarṣano'cyuta 114
Sanskrit 2, 17, 20, 95, 96, 97, 102, 107
Śānti Parva 6, 34, 113, 135
Saptaidhāh 114
Saptajihvāḥ 114
Saptaliṅga 102
Sapta Ṛíshi 101, 119, 120, 126
Saptasíndhu 24, 98
Sáraswatī 24, 98
Saros 10, 62, 90
Ṡatápatha Brāhmaṇa 4, 9, 33, 59, 65, 88, 91, 112, 129, 130, 134
Satī 56
Seals 94, 95, 103
Seasons 4, 18, 30, 88
Second millennium 95, 96, 103, 104, 122, 123
Serpent 10, 53, 54, 55, 56, 103, 123
Ṡesanāga 107
Seven deities 102
Seven Horses 28
Seven mothers 102
Seven sages 101, 102, 126, 129
Seven seeds 102
Seven stars 101
Seven wives 101
Siddhântic 33, 35, 37
Sidereal month 87, 90
Śíkhā 80
Ṡikhaṇḍi 119
Síndhu 24, 98
Sindshar 80
Siṉhavāhanī 135
Ṡipiviṣṭah 114
Sītā 128
Ṡiva 40, 54, 55, 56, 57, 61, 62, 64, 94, 97, 102, 115, 133, 159
Sky 5, 16, 27, 29, 30, 53, 55, 56, 126
Solar calendar 86; eclipse 35, 57, 61, 62, 66, 117, 120, 127; radiation 51, 56
Solar system 5, 46, 47, 111, 113, 115
Sóma 27, 29, 30, 40, 45, 46, 47, 51, 56, 87, 89, 96, 99, 109, 112, 122
Sphericity 17, 25, 57
Spica 135
Ṡṛiṅga 47
Ṡrīvatsa 114
Ṡrīvatsavaksha 114
Star map 88
Stars 16, 34, 35, 37, 49, 66
Sthāṇu 102, 113
Sthira 113
Stonehenge 24
Sudarśana 111, 114
Sumerians 34, 59, 82, 85, 86, 93, 103
Sumerian tradition 82
Summer solstice 65, 73, 74, 88, 110, 111, 119, 120, 126
Sun 4, 5, 8, 9, 10, 15, 16, 17, 18, 19, 26, 27, 28, 29, 30, 31, 32, 33, 34, 35, 37, 39, 41, 42, 43, 45, 46, 47, 48, 49, 51, 53, 54, 55, 57, 60, 61, 63, 65, 66, 72, 74, 87, 88, 101, 102, 103, 107, 110, 111, 112, 113, 114, 115, 119, 120, 126, 159
Supernova 36
Sūrya 20, 96, 159
Sūrya Siddhânta 10
Svâhā 101
Swastika 98, 100, 105, 123, 131
Synodic month 30, 86, 88, 89, 90, 107, 108
Syria 82

Taittirīya Brāhmaṇa 73, 74, 91
Taittirīya Saṃhita 73, 91, 134
Tajikistan 95, 104, 122
Takshaśila 121
Tāraḥ 114
Tāraka 56
Taurus 135
Tepe Hissar III 95, 122
Tiger 103
Tilak, B.G. 64, 65, 91
Tishyà 64, 65, 66, 67, 71, 72, 127, 128
Togolok 95, 96, 99, 101

Tortoise 53, 54, 55, 111, 128, 129
Tretā Yugá 60, 66, 127
Trilocana 55
Tripurâri 55, 56, 122
Triśaṅku 52, 126
Trivikrama 110
Tugra 82
Turkey 23, 67, 71, 77, 117
Turkistan 121
Turkmenistan 94, 95, 101, 103, 117, 122
Tushāra 11, 121
Twilight 5, 27, 28, 29, 30, 51, 54, 56, 60, 110

Ujjain 38, 132
Ukraine 75
Universe 16, 33, 35, 36, 39, 52, 54, 55, 115
Upanishad 19, 23, 35, 36, 98, 105
Uranus 20, 121
Urfa 77, 82
Uttarâyaṇa 119

Vaijayanta 111, 114
Vaikuṇṭha Ekādaśí 126
Vájra 51, 110
Vālmikī 52, 55
Vāman 54, 109, 113, 115
Vána Parva 62
Vanamāli 114
Varāhamihira 35, 37, 105
Váruṇa 20, 86, 96, 99, 100
Vásisṭha 17, 127
Vāsuki 10, 54, 110
Vásus 31, 32, 90, 119, 120, 129
Vāyu Purāṇa 53
Vedânta 25
Vedas 17, 23, 24, 25, 26, 30, 31, 36, 43, 98, 126
Vedic 2, 3, 4, 7, 11, 24, 25, 29, 35, 55, 61, 80, 81, 82, 83, 85, 86, 89, 90, 91, 92, 96, 97, 104, 105, 106, 107, 125, 127, 132, 133, 136; civilization 68, 75, 92, 105, 136; deities 82, 96; priest 8, 69, 80, 81, 104, 128, 160; seers 65; traditions 82
Venus 15, 16, 18, 19, 26, 27, 40, 41, 46, 47, 48, 51, 56, 72
Vernal equinox 60, 61, 62, 65, 66, 71, 73, 74, 75, 128, 129, 130, 134, 135
Vīrabhadra 54, 159
Virgo 135
Víśākha 73, 101, 112, 126, 134
Víshṇu 10, 18, 27, 45, 49, 51, 52, 54, 55, 103, 109, 110, 111, 113, 114, 115, 159, 160
Víshṇu Purāṇa 5, 53, 106, 111, 112, 113, 118, 120, 133
Víshṇu Sahásranāma 49, 113
Viśvāmitra 17, 52, 126, 127
Vṛikas 105
Vṛitrá 27, 29, 51, 54
Vyāsa 117, 118, 119, 123, 135
Vyāsakuṭa 73

Winter solstice 65, 72, 73, 74, 88, 91, 110, 118, 119, 126, 127, 128, 130, 132, 134, 135

Xixiang 11
Xuan hua 88

Yahiveh 107
Yahva 107
Yajur Veda 34, 80, 87
Yavanas 121
Yarkand 87, 123
Yoga 131; posture 94; sutras 65
Yugá 10, 60, 65, 114, 127, 129, 132
Yugādikṛit 114

Zarasthustra 67
Zend avesta 67
Zeus 121
Zodiac 1, 2, 15, 111, 133; belt 15, 18, 27; sign 2, 19
Zoroastrian 67, 82, 83, 102, 128